SIGNATURE PAGE

TO

_____

"BECAUSE I KNOW GOD CAN DO THE IMPOSSIBLE"

FROM

_____

AUTHOR'S SIGNATURE

_____

WORDS OF PRAISE FOR
TWO AND A HALF ACRES OF FAITH

For over two decades, I've had the privilege of knowing Jay Miller and witnessing his unwavering faith in action. In *Two and a Half Acres of Faith*, Jay shares powerful personal stories of how big dreams, perseverance, and trust in God have shaped his family's life and legacy. This book is a heartfelt reminder that even when dreams seem to die, faith can resurrect them. Jay's journey will inspire you to hold on, trust God, and never give up on what He's placed in your heart.

—Dr. Dave Martin
Best Selling Author of *12 Traits of the Greats*

Those two and a half acres changed my life and became the foundation for my ministry that spanned over forty years. This book will deeply touch your heart. As you read, you'll find yourself inspired and encouraged by a story of faith, perseverance, and God's provision. Many readers will relate to its powerful message and feel compelled to share how it has stirred their own faith. It's a beautifully told story and one that will stay with you long after you turn the final page.

—Pastor Clint Brown
Senior Pastor of Judah Church, Orlando, FL
Writer of five #1 gospel charting songs
with the 2023 #1 song of the year
Grammy, Stellar, and Dove nominated artist

Jay offers a unique perspective, having witnessed his parents faithfully follow God's call while living out their vision. With a front-row seat to their authentic faith, he now leads the very church and school they planted, carrying forward their legacy. This inspiring story will strengthen your faith and encourage you to pursue the God-sized dreams in your own life.

—Scott Bledsoe
Multi-campus Pastor, Household of Faith Church, Gonzales, LA

A must-read for anyone seeking to strengthen their faith, *Two and a Half* Acres of Faith offers a front-row seat to how God speaks and performs miracles in our lives. This book will challenge you to trust, believe, and follow God's voice while inspiring you to step out in bold faith. Reading it made me want to jump in my car and drive down the interstate, searching for new territory in my life and city, fueled by faith in a God who still moves mountains.

—Derek Capello
Senior Pastor, Northridge Church, White House, TN

Jay masterfully weaves together miraculous stories and profound insights into the God who makes the impossible possible. This book is for anyone who has struggled to hear God's voice, faced despair in times of adversity, or felt weary in their journey of faith. Prepare to be inspired, encouraged, and reminded of the power of unwavering trust in God.

—Stuart Sherrill
Superintendent of the Heartland Conference of the IPHC

This story will stir your faith and remind you of a God who desires to work through each of us to build strong, Christ-centered families. Jay masterfully chronicles a legacy of faith, sharing lessons, miracles, and challenges that will leave you inspired to ask yourself one powerful question: What will you do with your two and a half acres?

—Jeff Ables
Senior Pastor, Crossroads Church, Lafayette, LA

I've had the privilege of knowing Jay and the entire Miller family for over forty years. Jay and I share many things in common, including the blessing of raising five sons. Today, our sons—many serving in ministry—are deeply connected and work together to impact the same city for Christ. Nothing is more fulfilling than seeing your children wholeheartedly serve the Lord, but witnessing the next generation come together to build God's kingdom is truly priceless and a testament to the legacy of faith the Millers have lived and shared.

–Pastor Jacob Aranza
Multi-Campus Senior Pastor, Our
Savior's Church, Lafayette, LA

Like any great book, Jay Miller brought me into the story. I felt like I was riding along in the Chevelle and holding my breath as he recounted the courtroom experience with his parents. I believe Jay's book will inspire people to stretch their faith, walk in obedience, and dream big!

—Brant LaFleur
Property Manager/Owner, New Heritage Properties,
Cornerstone Rental, Arnaudville, LA

When I sat down to read *Two and a Half Acres of Faith*, I was blown away. Remarkable! This book will stir your faith and bring hope to those who have faced shattered dreams or life's unexpected challenges. Page by page, it leads readers to the unshakable hope and restoration found only in Jesus. If you're looking for encouragement, inspiration, and a reminder of God's faithfulness, this book is for you.

—Pastor Jay Coleman
Multi-campus Senior Pastor of Journey
Church, Denham Springs, LA

From the moment you open this book, you'll be captivated. Just two chapters in, I couldn't put it down, and my wife, Erica, felt the same. It spoke directly to where we are in this season of life. We can't wait to see how God uses this powerful story to inspire and change lives. It's a book that will touch your heart and strengthen your faith.

—Grant and Erica Gondron
Business Owner of Judice Services, Lafayette, LA

I'm not known to be an avid reader. However, I found myself eagerly turning the pages, captivated by the Miller family's unwavering trust in God's plan. Their story may have begun on two and a half acres, but through their faith and vision, their impact is beyond measure. This book will inspire you to see how faith can transform not just a family but an entire community—and how God's plans for us are always greater than we can imagine.

—Devin Lantier
Superintendent of Lafayette Christian Academy

We, the five Miller Boyz, hold this book close to our hearts because we are living its legacy. The story it tells is our story, and even now, new chapters are being written right before our eyes. Dad, thank you for your unwavering faithfulness to your calling and to our family. Your steady guidance carried us through our challenging teenage years, and your belief in us inspired us to see the potential God placed within us. You've modeled what it means to live with faith and vision, and now we are seeking to write our very own chapters in the spirit of *Two and a Half Acres of Faith*. We honor you, Dad, for the incredible life you've lived and the legacy you've given us to carry forward.

—The Miller Boyz (Sterling, Regan, Jansen, Micah, Britt)
Sons of Jay and Tessy Miller

Jay, your storytelling is so vivid and captivating that it held my full attention—a rare feat when I read! Your writing brings this incredible story to life, allowing readers to truly see and feel it. This book is heart-wrenching, compelling, and filled with faith. I am confident it will inspire and encourage both the faithful and those seeking hope. It's a powerful testament to the impact of trusting God throughout every season of life.

—Gene and Blanche Mills
President, Louisiana Family Forum, Baton Rouge, LA

Cover design by: Sara Young
Cover photo by: Jansen Miller

ISBN: 978-1-964794-27-3   1 2 3 4 5 6 7 8 9 10

Printed in the United States of America

TWO AND A HALF ACRES OF FAITH

How Faith Builds When Dreams Crumble

JAY S. MILLER

CONTENTS

Preface xv

Acknowledgments xix

Fifty Years of Faith: A Tribute to Our Founders 21

Why Read *2.5 Acres of Faith?* 23

Introduction 25

CHAPTER 1. **Just One Word**..27

CHAPTER 2. **Just Sixty Dollars and a Dream** 37

CHAPTER 3. **All I Want Is a Family** 47

CHAPTER 4. **The Dream Is Dead** 55

CHAPTER 5. **One Step at a Time** 63

CHAPTER 6. **Mom, Look, I Can Walk Again!** 73

CHAPTER 7. **Finally, a Family!**..................................81

CHAPTER 8. **"You Have Thirty Days"** 91

CHAPTER 9. **No One but Jesus**..................................101

CHAPTER 10. **Work Your Dream**..................................111

CHAPTER 11. **My Two Miracle Babies** 121

CHAPTER 12. **If My Mom Dies** 131

CHAPTER 13. **What Will You Pass Down?** 141

CHAPTER 14. **When Prayers Don't Work** 151

CHAPTER 15. **I'm in Hawaii** **159**

CHAPTER 16. **Happy Mother's Day, Jean!** **167**

CHAPTER 17. **We Built a Family** **175**

About The Family Church 187

About Lafayette Christian Academy 189

Author Bio... 191

PREFACE

What a journey it has been. At fifty-three years old, looking back on over three decades of ministry, family, and life, I can confidently say that God has been faithful through it all. As a miracle baby born to Sterling and Jean Miller, my very existence is a testimony to the goodness of God. Scripture says in Jeremiah 1:5, *"Before I formed you in the womb I knew you, before you were born I set you apart"*—I can truly attest to this truth in my life.

Growing up in a home where faith was lived out daily set the foundation for my life. I graduated from Lafayette Christian Academy in 1988, played basketball in college, and even had a stint in semipro football. At the age of twenty-three, I married my high school sweetheart, Tessy, and together, we've been on an incredible journey of faith, family, and ministry. One of my greatest joys has been raising our five boys and watching them grow, compete, and excel—not just in sports but in life. Psalm 127:3 reminds us, *"Children are a heritage from the Lord, offspring a reward from him."* Indeed, my boys have been my greatest reward and teachers. They've shown me what it means to lead with love, patience, and faith.

The journey of ministry began for me in 1990 as a junior high youth pastor, and what a ride it's been! From those early days, God has expanded my territory in ways I never could have imagined. In 2007, I completed my undergraduate degree at Southwestern Christian University in Bethany, Oklahoma, while continuing to serve in ministry. Over the years, I have worn many hats—pastor, husband, friend, president, entrepreneur, developer—but the titles I cherish most are father and now, Poppa Jay.

My five sons have been the biggest part of my life's story. Watching them compete in high school sports, and several at the college level, was amazing. Now, they're competing in the game of life, and they are winning. One of my life's goals was to raise them to be God-fearing men, to fulfill their God-given abilities, and I've had a front-row seat to their journey. I get to work alongside three of them every day, and it brings me such joy to see them shine at their craft. As Proverbs 22:6 (NKJV) says, *"Train up a child in the way he should go, And when he is old he will not depart from it."*

Over the past thirty years, I have been blessed to travel the world, serving alongside incredible leaders, including being part of John Maxwell's *Million Leaders Mandate* and training over 1 million leaders globally. I've spent many years in Southern Africa, teaching and training leaders. But no matter where my travels have taken me, my heart has always been rooted in family.

I have enjoyed every season of my life, but I truly believe that I am living out the best season ever. Yes, life still has its challenges, disappointments, and tough decisions to make, but the joy in my heart as I reflect on what God has done in me and through me at every stage fills my life with faith, contentment, and gratitude. Philippians 1:6 reminds us, *"He who began a good work in you will carry it on to completion until the day of Christ Jesus."* This verse resonates deeply with me, knowing that the work God started in me is far from finished. Every chapter, every challenge, every victory has been part of His greater plan. I walk forward with confidence and joy, knowing He isn't done yet.

Tessy, my partner through it all, has been my anchor. Together, we've raised our boys, and now, as grandparents, we are entering a new chapter. The days of parenting from inside our home are coming to a close, but the sound of little feet running through our house as Poppa Jay and Amie is a new joy we cherish.

As I reflect on this incredible journey, I am reminded of God's faithfulness at every turn. I step into this new season with great expectation, trusting that the best is yet to come, for His plans for us are always greater than we could ever imagine.

As you read *2.5 Acres of Faith*, my hope is that you will be inspired to see God's hand in your own life, no matter how small or impossible the dream may seem. This story is about more than land or buildings—it's about faith, perseverance, and the unfolding of God's purpose in ways we often cannot see at first. If there is one thing I hope you take away, it is this: God can do the extraordinary through ordinary people who are willing to trust Him step by step. My prayer is that *2.5 Acres of Faith* ignites a spark of faith in your heart to dream big, trust God fully, and watch as He exceeds your expectations in ways you never imagined.

ACKNOWLEDGMENTS

To Sterling and Jean Miller, the true giants of faith in my life. You have passed on a legacy that I carry with pride. Your resilience, your unwavering commitment to God, and your pioneering spirit in Acadiana have left an indelible mark on me and countless others. You never quit, even when the road was hard, and the dream seemed distant. I stand on your shoulders, forever grateful for your courage and example.

To Tessy, my high school sweetheart, my partner for over thirty years, and the mother of our five incredible boys—there are no words that can truly capture the depth of my gratitude and love for you. You are the heartbeat of our home, the true definition of motherhood. Your strength, wisdom, and unconditional love have shaped our family in ways only eternity will reveal. Thank you for walking this journey with me, hand in hand, through every season.

To my five Boyz, my greatest teachers. You have shaped me more than you'll ever know. Watching you grow, face challenges, and stand tall in a world that seems upside down at times, has shown me what true manhood looks like. You embody integrity, strength, and courage. I am beyond proud of the men you've become, and I know the world is better because of you.

To my three beautiful daughters-in-law, what a gift you are to our family. You complement our family perfectly, and I love the way you love my boys. I prayed for each of you long before we met, and God answered those prayers in ways more beautiful than I could have imagined. You add grace, joy, and beauty to our family in ways that leave me in awe. Thank you for making our family complete.

To The Family Church, my family of faith, the most amazing group of people in the world. For over twenty-two years, you have believed in me, supported me, and stood by my side as we've navigated life together. Pastoring you has been one of the greatest honors of my life. You make my life richer, my purpose clearer, and my heart fuller. Thank you for trusting me with your lives, your families, and your faith journey.

To the Lafayette Christian Academy staff and families, my first love. What a privilege it has been to walk these halls, to look into the eyes of your children, and to see the limitless potential they carry. What an incredible calling we share! There is no greater joy than seeing the seeds of faith planted in the next generation. The best is yet to come—watch and see what God will do!

Special thanks to Mark Lagrone, a faithful member of The Family Church for many years. You rekindled the flame for me to sit down and write *2.5 Acres of Faith*. I will always love you for that gentle push. Thank you for being the nudge I needed to share this story with the world.

Thank you all for being part of this incredible journey with me. I am forever grateful.

FIFTY YEARS OF FAITH:
A TRIBUTE TO OUR FOUNDERS

To the readers of *2.5 Acres of Faith,*

As you read these pages, you're not just encountering stories—you're stepping into the heart of a legacy that has spanned over fifty years of unwavering faith, sacrifice, and perseverance. The Family Church (TFC) stands today because of two extraordinary individuals whose faith in God became the foundation for everything we now see. At the center of that story is my mother, Jean Miller.

Jean was far more than a pastor's wife—she was the quiet strength behind the scenes, the heartbeat of our family, and the steady hand that helped guide the vision of this church. For over fifty-two years, she faithfully stood beside my father, Sterling Miller, through every season, trial, and triumph. Her love for people was limitless. She had the rare ability to make everyone feel like they mattered, no matter who they were or where they came from. Her Women's Bible Study impacted thousands, drawing women closer to God through her wisdom, deep love for the Word, and passion for the kingdom. She taught not just with words but with her life—her faith was a beacon of hope for so many.

Even when her time at TFC came to an end, Jean's work for the kingdom was far from finished. She went on to help build three more churches before her passing on January 4, 2012. Her work on this earth may have concluded, but the seeds she planted continue to bear fruit, impacting lives to this day.

Then there's my father, Sterling. At eighty-six years old, he still attends TFC every Sunday, sitting faithfully in the back row, greeting those around him with a kind word and a smile. He prays for me, Tessy, and our boys daily. Every morning, without fail, he calls to check on the ministry and our family, and every Thursday, we spend the day running errands and having lunch together. He always tells me how much he loved my sermon, though I'm not sure how much he hears from the back these days. But that's the thing about my father's faith—it's not about hearing; it's about presence, consistency, and showing up. After fifty-one years, he's still living out the legacy he and my mother started in 1973.

What my parents built was never about brick and mortar—it was about people, faith, and trust in a God who could do the impossible. They endured heartbreak, loss, and seasons where the dream seemed out of reach. But through it all, they held onto their faith, trusting that God's plan was greater than their circumstances. They didn't just build a church—they built a legacy that has touched countless lives and will continue to do so for generations.

As you reflect on these Fifty Years of Faith, my hope is that their story will inspire you. No matter where you are, no matter what you face, know that faith has the power to move mountains. Just as my parents did, trust God, step out in faith, and watch what He will do.

I will always love you, Mom and Dad.

Jay S. Miller

WHY READ 2.5 ACRES OF FAITH?

*T*wo and a Half Acres of Faith is a story of hope, resilience, and the power of dreams. Written to inspire, this book invites you to reignite the dreams you thought were lost and find hope for the future.

In honor of my parents, Sterling and Jean Miller, who passed down a legacy of unwavering faith to me, my family, and my five sons, I share the journey of their lives—stories of faith, loss, and miracles that I both witnessed firsthand and heard retold over the course of five decades.

As you read, I hope these real-life stories of triumph through adversity will encourage you to keep pressing forward, even when the path seems uncertain.

Let this book be a reminder that no dream is too far out of reach. My prayer is that through these pages, your heart will be stirred, your hope renewed, and your dreams brought back to life.

INTRODUCTION

T he stories within these pages are not mere tales—they are truths. Some have been whispered to me over the years, entrusted like sacred treasures. Others, I have witnessed from the front row, standing in awe as God's hand worked through impossibilities. Life is unpredictable, full of moments that test the core of who we are and what we believe. *Two and a Half Acres of Faith* is the story of such a journey—a journey that will grip your heart and stir your soul.

Sterling and Jean Miller had every reason to give up. After eight miscarriages and the stillbirth of their son, Mathias, it seemed as though their dream of having a family was gone forever. Each loss was a heavy blow, leaving them questioning everything they thought they knew about hope, faith, and the goodness of God. How could a loving God allow so much pain?

But the story doesn't end there. With nothing more than a promise from God and sixty dollars in their pocket, Sterling and Jean did the unthinkable. They packed up and moved to a small, unassuming two and a half acre plot of land in Lafayette, Louisiana—a place that, to the world, held no future. Yet, it was here that they planted the seeds of a ministry that would grow beyond anything they could have imagined. What seemed like barren soil would soon flourish with life as faith brought forth miracles they had only dreamed of.

This book isn't just a story about land, or even about a church. It's about the relentless power of faith to transform our darkest moments into something beyond our wildest dreams. It's about trusting God when the world says all is lost and daring to believe in a miracle when nothing seems possible.

As you read, you'll notice the chapters are not written in chronological order. Life seldom unfolds in a straight line, and neither does this story. But piece by piece, as you turn the pages, a tapestry of God's faithfulness will emerge. You'll find yourself walking with Sterling and Jean through the darkest valleys, feeling the weight of their shattered dreams. But just as they did, you'll see how God meets us in our brokenness—how even in the silence, faith stirs beneath the surface, waiting to break through.

You'll ask yourself: What would I do in the face of such loss? Could I hold on to faith long enough to see the impossible unfold? And what if, like Sterling and Jean, the story that seems over is only just beginning? The answers to these questions may surprise you, and the journey will change the way you see faith forever.

CHAPTER I

JUST ONE WORD

In 1973, the I-10 construction of the Atchafalaya Basin Bridge, connecting Baton Rouge to Lafayette, had finally been completed.

It was a scorching, humid Sunday afternoon, following church service, when Sterling Miller, his wife Jean, and their two little ones, JoBeth and Jay, set out on a journey. JoBeth was four, Jay just three, and together, they were headed for a memorable drive across the newly expanded I-10 corridor over the Louisiana swamps.

Their adventure began at the Crowley Exchange, traveling east down Interstate 10. They were eager to see the marvel of the eighteen-mile bridge, suspended seventy feet above the swamp waters. As they drove in their '66 Chevy Chevelle wagon, the windows rolled down, they couldn't help but be mesmerized by the sweeping views of the freshly completed bridge, a feat of engineering that had been long-awaited.

After the eighteen-mile crossing, they pulled into a small coffee shop, refueling themselves for the drive back. Now heading west, they'd get to experience the same bridge from a new vantage point, catching glimpses of the sprawling wetlands once more.

Sterling and Jean were no strangers to small-town life, both born and raised in the rural regions of Iota and Jennings, Louisiana. They hailed from a place called Miller French, a community where French was still the language of the home, and people clung tightly to what mattered—family, food, and their love for one another.

As they made their way back across the bridge, they passed the overpass in Lafayette and peered down at the vast open land below. Acres of untouched soil stretched out before them, dotted with two small farmhouses, and a gravel road running through the middle. Horses grazed nearby, alongside sheep, goats, and a few cows. It was serene and peaceful—a sight that struck a deep chord in their hearts.

At that moment, something stirred inside Sterling. A nudge, subtle yet unmistakable, as though the quiet voice of God Himself was speaking to him. "Sterling, I'm calling you to Lafayette, Louisiana. I want you to start a church, a life-giving church, and help pioneer Christian education in southwest Louisiana."

His heart leaped. It was more than a thought—it was direction, vision, a divine mandate. But now what? What was the next step?

Have you ever had a moment like that? Some may call it an encounter. Others might call it a God-sized revelation. It's more than just a fleeting thought; it's a moment that stops you in your tracks. Something hits your spirit so hard that it's as if time itself pauses. Your heart races, your mind swirls, and deep inside, you know this is different. This is beyond your imagination or daydreams—this is divine. You can sense it, almost as if the very voice of God is speaking directly to your heart.

Perhaps you've had dreams before—visions of something greater—but they felt like distant hopes, always just out of reach. No movement. No clear direction. But now, this one thought, this one spark, explodes in your heart like a fire. You know without a doubt that this isn't just another idea. It's a calling, a whisper from God Himself, inviting you into something bigger, something beyond your own capacity to even imagine. You can't shake it, no matter how hard you try. It's a moment so heavy with divine purpose that you know the Creator of the universe is personally calling you to step out in faith.

But here's the question: what do you do when this happens? Do you wait, hoping the weight of it will fade, convincing yourself it was just a passing feeling? Or do you begin to explore, to seek, to knock on every door before you? Do you dare to believe that God is leading you into something greater?

What happens when the road gets difficult, when uncertainties and roadblocks appear, and you realize that the dream is far bigger than your resources, your abilities, or your plans? What do you do when you come face to face with the impossible?

That's the moment of decision. Do you shrink back, or do you lean into the very heart of God, trusting that He who gave the vision will also provide the way? Because if it's truly from God, the obstacles aren't there to stop you—they're there to strengthen your faith. They remind you that what God is calling you to is not something you can accomplish on your own. It's something that requires His power, His provision, and His presence every step of the way.

When you realize this, you understand that it's not just about the dream. It's about trusting the God who gave it to you and walking in obedience, no matter what lies ahead.

As they drove the final thirty miles back to their home in Church Point, Sterling's mind raced. The heat and humidity were the least of his concerns now. His heart pounded, his thoughts spinning. He had no idea that in that moment, everything was shifting. His life, his family's future, and his legacy were being shaped, all from a single word from God.

Just one word from God can change everything. It can alter your path, redirect your course, and set the future in motion.

Sterling couldn't get Isaiah 55:11 out of his mind: "When My word goes forth, it will not return to Me empty; it will accomplish what I desire and achieve the purpose for which I sent it" (author paraphrase).

But what was next? More would come. It would take faith, patience, and a lot of hard work.

This was just the beginning.

Over the past thirty years of my journey, one truth has become crystal clear: no matter what season of life you're in, you must have a direct word from God for that moment. Whether you're navigating the complexities of singleness, the joys and challenges of marriage, finding yourself single again, or walking through the grief of widowhood, one thing remains constant—you need a word. Maybe you're stepping into a new job, embracing a fresh opportunity, charting a new course in your career, or even launching a new business. Whatever the season, I've learned that without a clear word from God, you're missing the most crucial piece of guidance.

JUST

ONE

WORD

FROM

GOD

CAN

CHANGE

EVERYTHING.

Life is unpredictable, and it doesn't ask permission to disrupt your plans. Problems will surface. Unforeseen circumstances will blindside you. Pain and discomfort—both physical and emotional—will show up uninvited. Distractions, often unwanted and unwelcome, will appear when you're already carrying more than you think you can bear. And they won't wait for a convenient time. These challenges will arise when you least expect them, when you feel least prepared, and when you desperately wish for peace and stability.

But none of this should come as a surprise. The Bible makes it plain: "In this world you will have trouble" (John 16:33). It doesn't tell us if trouble will come, but when. Yet, the same scripture also gives us reason to rejoice—because we have already overcome through Christ.

In every season of life—whether joyful or tumultuous, expected or unexpected—you need a word from God that is specific to where you are. All it takes is just one word. That word becomes your anchor. It grounds you when the winds of adversity blow hard and heavy. When distractions try to knock you off course, when the weight of life feels too much to carry, it's that divine word that steadies your soul.

Opposition will come. That's a given. Distractions will flood in. The burdens of life will press upon you, threatening to slow your progress or stop you altogether. But when you have a word from God, it will not only keep you focused, but it will also propel you forward. That word becomes your lifeline, your unwavering guide through the storms of life. It is what keeps you steady when everything around you feels uncertain. And it's that word that will see you through, no matter what the season brings.

So, as you move forward in your own journey, remember this: it's not just about getting through the season—it's about getting through it with a purpose, with vision, and with the firm assurance that God's word is your constant companion. Whatever comes, you can be sure that His word will never fail you.

On that Sunday afternoon drive home, Sterling knew without a shadow of a doubt that God had spoken. He had his marching orders, his divine direction. Everything changed. That word carried more weight than any plan or strategy he could have devised. It was a word that demanded obedience, a word that carried the very breath of heaven.

Now, let me ask you—what is *your* word? What is the word that God is speaking over your life in this very season? Do you have one? If not, it's time to get one. The Word of God is living, active, and sharper than any two-edged sword. It cuts through confusion, breaks chains of fear, and gives purpose to the chaos around you (Hebrews 4:12). But here's the thing—you can't afford to move forward without it. Life may seem like a series of mundane moments, but one word from God can transform your entire trajectory.

Maybe you're in a season of waiting, wondering, or even wrestling with what comes next. Perhaps you feel like you're walking in circles with no clear sense of direction. But don't stay there. Don't let another day go by without seeking the Lord for *your* word. God still speaks—He speaks in the stillness, He speaks in the storm, and He speaks in the everyday moments of life. And when He speaks, everything changes.

So, if you don't have a word for this season of your life, it's time to seek one with all your heart. Ask God, "What are You saying to me right now? What is Your plan for this season?" And then, listen. Wait. Tune your ear to the whisper of His voice.

Because when you have a word from God, you can face anything. You can walk through storms with peace, face mountains with faith, and navigate valleys with hope. A word from God gives you clarity in confusion, strength in weakness, and purpose in pain. It's not just a promise—it's a lifeline, a direction, and a declaration from heaven.

What word does God have for you right now? Do you have one for this season of your life? If not, seek it! Don't wait—press in, pray, and listen. God's direction is essential, and His Word will guide you through whatever lies ahead.

It only takes ONE!

WHEN

YOU HAVE

A WORD

FROM GOD,

YOU CAN

FACE

ANYTHING.

CHAPTER 2

JUST SIXTY DOLLARS
AND A DREAM

T he sun couldn't come up fast enough that Monday morning. It was the morning after an eighteen-mile Sunday drive, the morning after Sterling received a direct word from God. Sleep had evaded him all night long as he lay in bed, restless, watching the clock tick hour after hour. The excitement and anticipation wouldn't let him rest. The enormity of what he had felt stirred his soul, filling him with both excitement and fear.

He was nervous, yet confident. Filled with faith, yet battling an army of doubts. As the first rays of dawn crept into the sky, Sterling's thoughts swirled.

What if?

What if that wasn't God actually speaking to him yesterday? What if it was just his imagination, wishful thinking?

What if he couldn't find the piece of land that had captured his heart, the one he had seen nestled in the valley off Interstate 10 in Lafayette? What if it didn't even exist?

And even if it did exist, what if it wasn't for sale? What if this whole endeavor was a foolish waste of time—for him, for his family, for everything they had sacrificed?

And perhaps the greatest fear of all: what if his sixty dollars wouldn't be enough? How could a mere sixty dollars be the seed of something significant? The odds seemed stacked against him.

Have you ever counted yourself out because of the number in your bank account? Maybe you've looked at the skills you think are required, and you feel woefully inadequate as if the gap between where you are and where you need to be is too wide. Perhaps you feel like life hasn't made the deposits in you that you now need to draw from—like you were somehow overlooked, and you're lacking the tools, the resources, or the opportunities to even begin. And then there are the odds—they seem impossibly stacked against you, towering like giants in your path, taunting you to give up before you've even taken the first step.

But here's the truth: don't you dare discount yourself before the journey even starts.

God isn't asking you to have everything figured out. He's not waiting for you to have the perfect résumé, the ideal circumstances, or all the resources neatly lined up. He's looking for your willingness. Your faith. Your heart that says, "I will go, even if I feel unqualified." The story of Scripture is filled with men and women who started with nothing but a whisper from God and a heart full of faith. Gideon was hiding in fear, David was a shepherd boy, Moses could barely speak—and yet, God called each one of them not because of what they had, but because of who He is.

DON'T

YOU DARE

DISCOUNT

YOURSELF

BEFORE THE

JOURNEY

EVEN

STARTS.

So when the world tells you that you don't have enough—enough money, enough skill, enough confidence—remember, God isn't limited by your lack. He specializes in taking the impossible and making it reality. Where you see scarcity, He sees opportunity. Where you see weakness, He sees His strength made perfect. And where you see roadblocks, He is the God who parts seas.

The odds may be stacked against you, but they are never stacked against God. What matters is that *He* has called you, and when He calls, He equips. It's not about what you have in your hand right now—it's about who holds your hand. So don't count yourself out before the first step is even taken. Trust that if God has called you, He has already made provision for every need, even when you can't see it yet.

This journey isn't about your limitations—it's about His limitless power. Step forward in faith because God can take the little you have and use it to move mountains.

By 10 a.m. that Monday morning, Sterling could no longer sit idle. The dream was like a fire in his bones, and the only way to quench it was to move. The voice he heard the day before had birthed something in him, something he couldn't ignore. This was more than a whim; it was a calling. He had to pursue it. He had to know.

Without his family this time, he climbed into his car and drove back to Lafayette, praying every mile of the way. He prayed to find the land, prayed for confirmation, prayed that he hadn't misheard God's voice. And with each mile, the reality of his situation hung over him like a cloud. He had just sixty dollars in his pocket. Not nearly enough to buy land or make any kind of substantial move.

But that didn't stop him.

The twenty-five-mile drive from Church Point, Louisiana, to Lafayette felt like an eternity. It may have been just a half-hour trip, but for Sterling, it felt like the longest drive of his life. With every mile that brought him closer to Exit 101—the University exit in Lafayette—his heart beat faster. His thoughts raced faster still.

Could this be it? Could this be the day everything changed? Could this be the moment when a life-defining event would unfold? Or was he setting himself up for disappointment? Was this just another dead end, another season of waiting?

As he finally took Exit 101, turning onto University Avenue, his pulse quickened. And then, within just a quarter of a mile, he spotted it. A gravel road. It looked eerily familiar—the same road he had seen the day before, from that high perch on Interstate 10.

Normally, driving down a gravel road would be noisy and dusty, with the clatter of rocks and the cloud of dirt kicking up behind him. But not today. Today, Sterling couldn't hear any of that. The noise, the dust, everything faded into the background because, at that moment, something else was rising inside him: faith.

It was as if, on that Monday morning, faith itself found its voice.

Do you know that faith has a voice?

As Sterling drove down that half-mile stretch of gravel, something inside him shifted. It was more than just a feeling—it was the undeniable sense that he was being led, that God was guiding him toward something bigger than his doubts, bigger than his sixty dollars, bigger than anything he could comprehend.

FAITH

HAS A

DISTINCT

VOICE.

IT DOESN'T

SHOUT,

AND

IT DOESN'T

RUSH.

In my twenty years of pastoring, I've learned one thing above all else: faith has a distinct voice. It doesn't shout, and it doesn't rush. But it's clear, and it speaks with authority.

Just as Sterling heard it that day on Stone Avenue, I've heard it time and time again in my own life. The Bible says, "My sheep hear my voice" (John 10:27), and indeed, when you train your ear to hear the voice of faith, you'll begin to recognize it in every season, in every opportunity, and in every quiet moment of your life.

Opportunities come and go. Good ideas flood our minds. Business propositions, career moves, ministry endeavors—they all come knocking, often in rapid succession. Some seem urgent, others look promising. But I've learned to pause. I've learned to wait for the voice of faith.

God speaks through His Word, through pastors, through worship, and through stillness. Faith whispers where the world shouts. It nudges when the world pushes. And if we listen closely, we'll know when it's time to move forward—and when it's time to wait.

As Sterling navigated the gravel road that day, the voice of faith led him step by step. It was a voice that told him to keep moving, even when his circumstances seemed impossible. It was the voice of faith that drowned out the noise of doubt, fear, and inadequacy.

That Monday morning, as Sterling made his way down Stone Avenue, he realized something profound: faith wasn't just about the destination—it was about the journey. The voice of faith would lead him to that small plot of land, but more than that, it would lead him to a deeper understanding of God's provision, His timing, and His plans.

And just as Sterling discovered that day, we too must learn to hear that voice because, in the end, it's not just about having sixty dollars and a dream—it's about trusting that God can take something as small as sixty dollars and turn it into a story of faith, perseverance, and miraculous provision.

If faith truly has a voice, how do you hear it? Where do you find it?

Faith's voice doesn't always shout—it often whispers. It calls to you in the stillness of the night when doubts are loudest and fears creep in. It rises above the noise, quietly yet powerfully, urging you to trust in something greater than what your eyes can see. Faith's voice doesn't come from the chaos around you; it emerges from the depths within you, where the Spirit of God speaks to your soul.

So how do you hear it? You hear it when you silence the distractions, when you still your heart long enough to sense God's presence. You hear it when you open the Word, where every page echoes with the promises of a God who cannot lie. "So then faith *comes* by hearing, and hearing by the word of God" (Romans 10:17, NKJV). You hear it when you step out into the unknown, with nothing but trust in His name, and suddenly, faith's voice becomes louder than fear. It's in those moments when you face the impossible that faith speaks clearest, reminding you that with God, nothing is too great.

And where do you find it? You find it on your knees, in moments of surrender. You find it when you let go of control and trust God to make a way where there seems to be no way. You find it in the valleys, in the wilderness, in the quiet places of waiting—where faith is born not in the absence of struggle, but in the midst of it. "For we walk by faith, not by sight" (2 Corinthians 5:7, NKJV). Faith's voice is heard when you choose to believe before you see the outcome, when you stand firm on His promises, even when everything around you says otherwise.

Faith is not a feeling. It's not dependent on what your eyes can see or what your circumstances say. It's the quiet confidence in the One who spoke the universe into being, the One who holds your future in His hands. It's found in the moments when you're pressed on every side but choose to declare, "God is still faithful."

So, if faith truly has a voice—and it does—tune your heart to hear it. Seek it in His Word, find it in prayer, and listen for it in the everyday moments of life because faith always speaks, but it's up to you to quiet the noise and listen, and when you do, you'll hear it call you to deeper trust, greater hope, and a life lived beyond the limits of what you once thought possible.

FAITH

ALWAYS SPEAKS,

BUT

IT'S UP TO YOU

TO

QUIET THE NOISE

AND

LISTEN.

CHAPTER 3

ALL I WANT IS A FAMILY

In the autumn of 1956, at the start of her senior year, Jean Hunt's life took an unexpected turn. Her family was being transferred from the quiet town of Cameron, Louisiana, to the even smaller community of Iota, Louisiana. At seventeen, Jean had spent most of her life in the flat marshlands of Cameron, and the news of relocating, though only ninety miles away, felt like moving to a whole new world. Little did she know that this move to Iota High School would become the beginning of what is almost every little girl's dream—to one day marry, start a family, and become a mother.

Jean Miller was born on July 10, 1939, in the rural countryside of southwest Louisiana. Raised in a large family with seven siblings, Jean's upbringing was rooted in love, hard work, and faith. Even in the smallest moments of her childhood, she carried within her a quiet but fierce desire: to one day have a family of her own.

It wasn't long after settling into her new high school that the path to that dream began to reveal itself. It was January 1957, and the Christmas break had just ended. As Jean returned to the final stretch of her senior year, she walked out to recess with a handful of friends by her side. There, beneath the sprawling branches of a grand Louisiana live oak in the school courtyard, she spotted him—Sterling Miller. Tall, handsome, and standing confidently as if the world revolved around that moment. She didn't know it yet, but that simple encounter would change the course of her life.

Sterling was from a family as large as Jean's, also one of eight children. He shared her love for big families and quickly bonded with her over their shared values. As their relationship blossomed, the two began to dream together. What would life look like beyond graduation? What would it be like to build a home, a life, a future—together?

Have you ever had a dream so powerful, so consuming, that it filled your heart with hope and wonder? A dream that once felt distant, like a far-off star you could only admire from a distance, but now—now it's close enough that you can almost touch it? It's the kind of dream that keeps you awake at night, your heart racing with the thought of *What if?* What if this one thing could actually come to pass? What if that wild, impossible dream wasn't so impossible after all?

On May 17, 1957, the dreams that had once only been whispered in the hallways of Iota High finally took form, becoming something real—something they could touch. That Friday night, under the glow of dim lights and the weight of unspoken hope, Jean and Sterling walked hand in hand across the worn graduation stage in the old, creaking gymnasium. The air inside was thick and heavy, the loud hum of fans struggling to cool the sweltering Louisiana heat, but none of that mattered. The heat, the sweat, the noise—it was all a blur compared to the significance of this moment.

Just a few short months later, on August 4, 1957, Jean Hunt became Jean Miller, the wife of Sterling Miller. Her childhood dream was now beginning to unfold. Sterling had already secured a job in the oil fields of South Louisiana, working long hours in Evangeline Parish. The couple moved into a modest shotgun house in the small, tight-knit community of Miller French, where Jean picked up odd jobs to contribute to their new life together. Their love for each other and for the family they envisioned sustained them through long days and humble beginnings.

In May of 1959, the moment Jean had longed for her entire life finally arrived. It wasn't just an ordinary day—it was the day when the deepest desire of her heart was fulfilled. After weeks of waiting, wondering, and praying, the local doctor delivered the news that Jean and Sterling had been hoping for. She was pregnant with their first child. The words seemed to hang in the air, surreal and powerful, and in that instant, Jean's entire world shifted.

Her heart swelled with joy, a joy so deep and overwhelming that it brought tears to her eyes. This was the moment she had dreamed of since she was a little girl, the dream that had filled her prayers and her quiet thoughts. All she had ever wanted was to become a mother, to hold a child of her own, and now, that dream was no longer a distant hope—it was real. She placed a hand on her stomach, imagining the tiny life growing inside her, and in that moment, the promise of motherhood became something she could almost feel, something tangible.

For Jean, this was more than just the start of a pregnancy—it was the beginning of a dream that had been rooted deep in her soul for as long as she could remember. The image of a family, of children running through the house, of little feet pattering on the floor, had always been the picture of her future. Now, that future was within reach.

She and Sterling, though young and with little more than love and faith to their name, embraced this new chapter with hopeful anticipation. They knew the road ahead wouldn't be easy. Their finances were tight, their resources limited, and their incomes barely enough to cover the basics. But none of that mattered—not now, not in the face of this miracle. What they lacked in material wealth, they more than made up for in faith and love. They would make this work. They had to.

The challenges ahead seemed small compared to the excitement that filled their hearts. Jean could already picture herself holding their baby, rocking him or her to sleep, and Sterling, who was usually quiet about his emotions, had a sparkle in his eye that spoke of the hope and dreams he held for their growing family. Together, they would face whatever came next, step by step, with the unwavering belief that God had brought them this far and would carry them the rest of the way.

At that moment, their world was full of promise. The life they had dreamed of building together was no longer just a hope—it was beginning, right there, inside Jean's womb. Every day from that moment forward would be filled with the joy of expectation, the wonder of knowing that soon, they would be parents. Soon, their family would grow, and the future they had always longed for would come to life.

However, life has a way of throwing unexpected curves. On the morning of July 14, 1959, Jean awoke in the middle of the night with a sharp, agonizing pain. Fear flooded her heart as the pain intensified, a terrible sign of something wrong with the child growing inside her. By the end of that day, Jean's dream was abruptly put on hold as her body rejected the pregnancy. She suffered a miscarriage.

In an instant, the future they had so carefully imagined crumbled into heartbreaking uncertainty. The excitement that once filled their hearts, the plans they had made, the joy they had nurtured—they all vanished, replaced by a deep, searing grief that seemed to swallow them whole. The dreams of a nursery, of a child's laughter filling their home, faded like a distant echo. The hope that had once been so bright now felt like an unbearable weight. They were left standing in the wreckage of their shattered dreams, unsure how to move forward in a world that suddenly felt so empty.

Sterling, who had always been her pillar of strength, walked into the hospital room at Jennings American Legion Hospital that evening. He found Jean lying there, her heart shattered, the weight of their loss heavy on her shoulders. He tried to offer her comfort, but the pain in his own heart was hard to hide. The sight of his wife, once so full of hope, now drowning in disappointment, was almost too much to bear.

For Jean, it wasn't just the loss of a child. It felt like the loss of a dream—a dream she had carried since she was a little girl, a dream that seemed so close, only to slip through her fingers at the last moment. The emotional pain far outweighed the physical suffering. The questions in her mind were relentless. Would she ever be able to conceive again? Was this a sign that her body could not carry a child to term? Would her dream of having a family be forever out of reach?

LIKE A FLOWER

PUSHING THROUGH THE

CRACKS IN THE

HARDEST GROUND,

HOPE BEGINS

TO GROW

IN PLACES

WE LEAST EXPECT.

We've all faced moments in life where our dreams seem to come crashing down, leaving us disoriented, heartbroken, and questioning everything we thought we knew. These are the moments that test our faith, challenge our hope, and force us to choose between giving up or pressing on.

For Jean, this was that moment.

But perhaps, this was just the beginning of an even greater story—one that couldn't yet be understood. While Jean lay in that hospital bed, broken and uncertain, life was not finished writing her story. The dream of family was still alive, though it would take time, faith, and perseverance to see it fully realized.

Sometimes, it is in the very depths of our darkest moments that the seeds of hope are quietly, almost imperceptibly, planted. In the midst of heartbreak, when the weight of sorrow feels unbearable and the future seems impossibly bleak, something stirs beneath the surface. Though we may not see it or feel it in that moment of despair, hope is taking root. It waits—patiently, silently—until the right time to emerge. Like a flower pushing through the cracks in the hardest ground, hope begins to grow in places we least expect. It may seem fragile at first, but in time, it will bloom into something stronger and more resilient than we ever imagined. For it is in those very moments of brokenness that God's hand gently places the seed of something new, something beautiful, preparing us for a future we cannot yet see.

As Jean and Sterling left the hospital, hearts heavy but hands still clasped tightly together, they held on to a promise that would guide them through the uncertain days ahead. We have each other; we will not give up. With these words echoing in their hearts, Jean and Sterling chose to believe that their story was far from over, that their dream of family would one day be fulfilled, even if they could not yet see how.

"For I know the plans I have for you," declares
the LORD, "plans to prosper you and not to harm
you, plans to give you hope and a future."
—Jeremiah 29:11

Let Jeremiah 29:11 serve as a powerful reminder of God's unwavering plan, even when life feels uncertain or painful. It reassures us that His promises are sure, and His purposes for our lives are always at work, even when we can't see the way forward.

This verse speaks of a future filled with hope, restoration, and blessing, offering comfort in times of doubt. It encourages us to place our faith in God's goodness, reminding us that setbacks and heartaches are not the end but rather part of His larger plan for our growth, peace, and ultimate prosperity. No matter how long it may take.

Sterling and Jean had no idea how that plan was about to unfold in the coming years. No one could have imagined it. After all, more than anything, all Jean ever wanted was a family.

CHAPTER 4

THE DREAM IS DEAD

July 14, 1959, was a day that left an indelible mark on the lives of Sterling and Jean Miller. It was the day Jean miscarried their first pregnancy—a heartbreaking end to a chapter that they had hoped would be the beginning of their family. The loss was profound, a heavy weight that settled into the silence of their home. Yet, even in the midst of their grief, the flicker of hope had not fully died.

That November, just a few months later, the same small-town doctor delivered unexpected news: Jean was pregnant again. The possibility of redemption from the heartache stirred within them once more. Could this be the moment they had prayed for? Could this pregnancy be different from the last? Their hearts, though still bruised, began to open to the fragile hope that perhaps this time, their dream of starting a family would finally come true.

With cautious optimism, Sterling and Jean quietly embraced the new life growing inside of her. They didn't share the news widely, afraid to speak their hopes aloud. The fear of repeating their past loss held them back from celebrating. After all, who could bear the weight of announcing a new pregnancy

only to have to endure public shame and sorrow if things
went wrong again?

They approached this second pregnancy with a delicate and
cautious hope. Every step was taken with great care, guided
by their doctor, and armed with the best medical advice available in the early 1960s. Jean followed every precaution, clung to
every instruction, and prayed with every fiber of her being. Yet,
despite all their efforts, despite the tender care with which they
approached this new life, Jean was once again awakened in the
middle of the night by a familiar and dreaded pain. The ache she
felt wasn't just in her body but in her soul—an all-too-familiar
grief stirring within her. By the time the sun set on that fateful
day, their second child was gone.

For most couples, this kind of heartbreak would be unbearable,
enough to shatter even the strongest of spirits. But for Sterling
and Jean, this was only the beginning of a long and agonizing
journey. Over the next six years, they would walk through this
nightmare not just once or twice, but six more times, enduring
a total of eight miscarriages. Eight times they felt the hope of
new life growing within them, only to have that hope snatched
away in the cruelest of ways.

Each time, they hoped that this one would be different.
Each time, they dared to believe that maybe, just maybe, this
pregnancy would be the one to carry their dream forward. But
with every loss, their hopes were dashed against the harsh
reality of yet another empty cradle. The pain grew deeper with
each miscarriage.

The world around them could not understand the depth of
their pain. With every loss, they carried not just the weight of

grief, but the burden of unanswered questions, of wondering why the very thing they longed for—the simple joy of becoming parents—seemed so impossibly out of reach.

The final pregnancy nearly took Jean's life. Due to the significant loss of blood, Jean's body went into shock, and her vital systems began to shut down. The medical team worked tirelessly to stabilize her, and miraculously, after a grueling effort on the operating table, they succeeded. Jean's life had been saved, but the ordeal had left her physically weak and emotionally shattered.

In the days that followed, Jean slowly began to regain her physical strength. Her body, bruised and battered, responded to rest and care, and with each passing day, she felt a little stronger. However, as her physical wounds healed, the emotional scars remained raw and unaddressed.

Though her body was recovering, the emotional and mental toll was only just beginning to unfold. She had endured the trauma of yet another miscarriage, the loss of her baby weighing heavily on her heart. While her physical strength returned, Jean now had to face the immense emotional weight of her grief, the feelings of loss, and the overwhelming uncertainty about her future as a mother. Each day became a battle between outward recovery and inward sorrow, as her mind and heart struggled to find peace amidst the pain.

The next phase of her healing would not be as straightforward as regaining physical strength. Jean knew she had to confront the lingering grief, the unanswered questions, and the emotional wounds that ran deeper than any physical injury. This emotional recovery would prove to be the more difficult and unpredictable path forward.

Unlike the others, this time she carried the baby into the second trimester, but the outcome was no less devastating. Their son, Mathias Miller, was stillborn. The doctor, knowing the toll it had taken on Jean's body and spirit, advised them to abandon the hope of having children naturally. The repeated complications had left Jean physically fragile and emotionally worn down.

How do you respond when you're told that the dream is over? When every voice around you says there is no recovery, no way forward? In those moments, it feels like the walls are closing in, like the hope you've been clinging to has been ripped from your hands. But as followers of Christ, we know that even when the world declares the end, God speaks a different word. He is the God of resurrection, the One who makes a way where there seems to be no way.

When we are told that the dream is over, we don't have to accept defeat. Instead, we turn to the One who holds all things in His hands. "For with God nothing will be impossible" (Luke 1:37, NKJV). What looks like the end to us is often just the beginning of a new chapter God is writing. Even when the road ahead seems impossible, we serve a God who can bring life out of death, hope out of despair, and victory out of what appears to be failure.

The world may say the dream is over, but God has the final word. And with Him, there is always a way forward.

THE TRIALS

YOU FACE

TODAY

ARE SHAPING

THE

TESTIMONY

YOU WILL

CARRY

TOMORROW.

Though Mathias had never taken a breath, Sterling and Jean decided to honor his life with a proper burial. They named him after Sterling's father and arranged for a small, private funeral at the Evangeline Cemetery. On a cold December morning in 1962, a few close family members and friends gathered to lay Mathias to rest. The funeral home staff carried a tiny white casket—no longer than a man's shoebox—holding their son's lifeless body. It was a painful sight that no parent should ever have to witness.

As the small casket was lowered into the ground, it felt to Sterling and Jean as though more than just their baby boy was being buried. With Mathias, they buried their dreams, their hopes of ever having a family of their own. It was not just a child that had been lost, but a future that had once seemed so bright.

When the funeral director finally sealed the vault lid on Mathias's grave, the world around Sterling and Jean seemed to fall into complete silence. The finality of it all was deafening. Their dream of becoming parents, of raising children together, was dead. There were no words to explain the depth of their sorrow. No thoughts could articulate the profound emptiness they felt. For them, the world had simply stopped turning.

Sometimes, life hits harder than we can anticipate, and for Sterling and Jean, it seemed to come all at once. The years of heartbreak, the repeated losses, and the crushing weight of burying their son left them questioning everything. How could their dream of family ever come true now? It felt as though God had turned His face away, leaving them to navigate the ruins of their shattered hopes alone.

Yet, Scripture tells us something different about suffering and loss. In 2 Corinthians 4:17, the apostle Paul speaks of our "momentary afflictions" and how they are preparing us for "an eternal glory that far outweighs them all." For Sterling and Jean, these years of loss felt like more than just momentary affliction. They felt final, as if the dream had truly died.

In the midst of your pain, it can be hard to see beyond the hurt, to understand why you are walking through such difficulty. But take heart—there is purpose in your pain. God never wastes a single tear, and though you may not see it now, He is working through every hardship to bring about something greater than you can imagine. The Bible reminds us, "And we know that in all things God works for the good of those who love Him, who have been called according to His purpose" (Romans 8:28).

Though the pain feels overwhelming, trust that God is refining you, strengthening you, and molding you into the person He's called you to be. The trials you face today are shaping the testimony you will carry tomorrow. Hold on to the truth that your suffering is not in vain—God is using it to fulfill His greater purpose in your life.

As they stood at Mathias's graveside, hearts heavy and broken, they could not see what lay ahead. But in the silence, there was a faint whisper—a reminder that their story was not over. Though the dream felt dead, perhaps, just maybe, it was only dormant, waiting for the right moment to bloom once again.

Sometimes, life feels like a long season of waiting, where progress seems slow and dreams seem distant. But just like a seed buried in the soil, there's growth happening beneath the surface. God is preparing you for the right moment to bloom once again.

Don't rush the process—trust that in His perfect timing, everything will fall into place. "He has made everything beautiful in its time" (Ecclesiastes 3:11). Your season of blooming is coming; just hold on in faith.

CHAPTER 5

ONE STEP AT A TIME

January 1973—Sterling Miller gripped the steering wheel of his old Chevy wagon as it rumbled down the gravel road on Stone Avenue. Dust billowed behind him, but inside his heart, something else stirred. As he passed by the familiar farmhouses, his faith was also being stirred. Something about this moment felt different, more urgent. It wasn't a passing thought or a whisper—it was beginning to feel like a mandate.

This was the beginning.

As Sterling reached the end of the gravel road, his wagon nestled into the cul-de-sac. He killed the engine and gazed at the expanse of land that lay before him. There were no "For Sale" signs, no advertisements that the land was available. But there was a tug in his spirit that had been growing since yesterday when he first saw this very land during a Sunday drive. His eyes scanned the two small farmhouses, one of them looking abandoned. A three-strand barbed wire fence ran parallel to the road, tied haphazardly to old wooden posts. He could hear the faint roar of cars speeding along the nearby I-10 highway, just five hundred feet away. But here, in this stillness, Sterling was standing on the edge of something far more significant than just land.

So, what was the next step?

He glanced down at his hand, where the weight of sixty dollars—the entirety of his savings—pressed into his palm. Sterling wasn't from Lafayette. He didn't know a single person in this growing Louisiana city. Yet, standing there with his meager savings, he felt an undeniable certainty. God had led him here. But now, with no real plan, no visible opportunity, and no connections, he asked himself: *What now?*

Sterling prayed, "God, what do I do now?"

In that quiet moment, he felt a gentle but profound answer rise in his spirit: *Whatever you have faith for, I'll give it to you.*

It wasn't a loud, booming voice; it was soft, like a whisper—but it was filled with certainty. The words reminded him of Luke 17:6, where Jesus said even faith as small as a mustard seed could move mountains, and right now, Sterling felt that mustard seed faith. He didn't have grand faith, at least not yet. He had sixty dollars, a wife, and two small children to care for. He had a dream but not much else.

Yet here he stood on the precipice of a new beginning.

Sterling began to walk. Each step he took stirred his imagination. The land was vacant, untouched, but in his mind, he began to see the outlines of a future—something tangible yet not fully formed. He envisioned a church building. A school. Classrooms. A parking lot. Office spaces. He stopped walking for a moment and turned his eyes toward the sky, "God, this is all the faith I have for today." He looked back down at the land and knew that this was where it would all begin.

IT'S

NOT ABOUT

HOW BIG

YOUR FAITH IS;

IT'S ABOUT

THE ONE

IN WHOM

YOUR FAITH

RESTS.

Have you ever felt like your faith was limited, like you didn't have enough to overcome the challenges in front of you? You're not alone. We've all experienced moments where our faith feels small, fragile, or even uncertain. But here's the beautiful truth: it's not about how big your faith is, it's about the One in whom your faith rests. Jesus said, *"If you have faith as small as a mustard seed, you can say to this mountain, 'Move from here to there,' and it will move. Nothing will be impossible for you"* (Matthew 17:20).

Even when your faith feels limited, God's power is limitless. The smallest act of faith in Him can move mountains. It's not about having perfect faith; it's about trusting a perfect God. So, when you feel like your faith isn't enough, remember that it's not the size of your faith, but the greatness of your God. Trust Him to do the impossible, even with what seems like the smallest bit of belief.

He stepped off a piece of the land, pacing slowly between the fence posts, the weight of the moment pressing on him with every step. His feet sank into the earth beneath him, but what felt even heavier was the faith stirring deep within his soul. Each step was deliberate, filled with a quiet determination and trust in the God who had called him here. The wind rustled through the grass, but all he could hear was the whisper of purpose echoing in his heart.

With every step, he could feel something greater unfolding. It wasn't just land he was measuring—it was a vision, a promise. He later calculated that the land he first stepped off measured just over one acre. One acre, just enough for the beginnings of something small, something humble. But as he stood there, surveying the ground beneath his feet, he knew—deep in his spirit—that one acre wouldn't be enough. The dream God had placed in his heart needed room to grow. So, with a quiet resolve, he kept walking, pacing off the area, marking the land bit by bit. His eyes scanned the horizon as he took slow, deliberate steps, believing that every inch of this land was part of God's plan.

As he reached the end, he stopped, breath catching in his throat. He had measured out 2.5 acres. It wasn't much by the world's standards, but to him, it was everything. It was a canvas for the future, a field for faith, a holy ground where the impossible could happen. He stood there, taking it all in, knowing in his heart—*this* was it. This land, these 2.5 acres, would be the foundation upon which God would build something far beyond what he could see at that moment. His heart swelled, not with pride, but with awe because he knew this wasn't just about land. It was about a divine promise, about stepping out in faith and trusting God to make the impossible real.

Sterling returned home that day, his mind racing. He remembered the story of Joshua marching around Jericho, circling it seven times before the walls came down. So, for the next seven days, he made the thirty-minute drive from Church Point back to Lafayette. He arrived at the same spot at the same time every day and stepped off that same tract of land. Each day, his faith grew stronger, his vision clearer.

On the seventh day, as Sterling arrived at the land once again, he noticed a man standing in the middle of the field. The man watched as Sterling got out of his car and approached the land he had been pacing off all week. As they met, the man spoke first: "Are you the guy who's been walking on my land every day?"

Sterling nodded. "Yes, sir, that's me."

The man introduced himself as Mr. Chester Robin, the owner of the very land Sterling had been stepping off. "Why are you walking here every day?" he asked.

Sterling took a deep breath and began to explain the vision God had given him—the church, the school, the future he saw for this land. Mr. Robin listened patiently, but when Sterling finished, he simply said, "Well, you've got a good plan, but this land isn't for sale."

Sterling wasn't discouraged. After all, he didn't even have the money to buy the land. "That's okay," he replied. "I don't have any money anyway."

And yet, that day, Sterling Miller bought land that wasn't for sale with money he didn't have. Mr. Robin was so moved by Sterling's faith and determination that he agreed to sell him the land. With a handshake and a sixty-dollar deposit, Sterling walked away the owner of 2.5 acres of land.

On April 22, 1973, something remarkable began on a small piece of land. That Easter Sunday, thirty-two people gathered for the first service of The Family Church (TFC) on the very ground that had been stepped off in faith just months before. The air was thick with anticipation, but no one in that room could have grasped the magnitude of what they were witnessing. To them, it was a humble beginning, a small gathering of believers united in their desire to worship God. But in heaven, it was the birth of something far greater—something that would grow beyond any-one's wildest expectations.

MAYBE

GOD

IS CALLING YOU

TO STEP OUT

ON YOUR OWN

"2.5 ACRES OF

FAITH."

That simple service on a patch of 2.5 acres was the seed planted in faith, and God was already preparing it to flourish. Just a year later, in August 1974, the doors of Lafayette Christian Academy opened, welcoming children from across the Acadiana area. What started as a small vision now had arms and legs, touching the lives of young ones and planting seeds of faith in a new generation.

And yet, that was just the beginning. What Sterling had once paced off in faith—the original 2.5 acres—has since become something so much greater. Today, TFC and Lafayette Christian Academy sit on over one hundred acres of thriving ministry. What began as a step of obedience and a spark of hope has turned into a flourishing, vibrant community of faith. That land, those once small steps, are now a living testament to what God can do with even the smallest acts of trust. It's more than just land; it's a living legacy of God's faithfulness, a miracle unfolding year after year.

That story—the one birthed on those 2.5 acres—isn't just about Sterling, or TFC, or even the thousands of lives now touched by the ministry. It's about what God can do when you take that first step of faith, no matter how small or uncertain it may seem. Maybe God is calling you to step out on your own "2.5 acres of faith." Maybe there's a dream, a vision, or a purpose that He's planted deep within you, just waiting for you to act in faith.

It's time to take the step. It's time to walk in obedience, to trust that what seems small now has the potential to grow into something far greater than you can imagine. Just like that small gathering of thirty-two people, maybe you're standing on the verge of witnessing God birth something extraordinary in your life. All it takes is a heart willing to step off the land of doubt and into the wide, open field of faith—where miracles wait just beyond the horizon.

CHAPTER 6

MOM, LOOK, I CAN WALK AGAIN!

Since the grand opening of TFC on Easter Sunday, 1973, Sterling and Jean Miller witnessed their dream start to take shape. What began as a humble congregation meeting in a retrofitted wood-framed shotgun house quickly started to grow. Almost weekly, new families joined the fold. What once seemed like an impossible vision, ridiculed and dismissed by some, was now beginning to flourish.

By modern standards, the original 2.5 acres on which they built their ministry would not amount to much. But back then, it was a miracle in itself. Sterling wore many hats in those days—pastor, school administrator, groundskeeper, builder, and even sewage overseer. Jean was no less involved, serving as Sunday school teacher, bus driver, children's pastor, and janitor. Together, they poured everything they had into this work. It was more than just dedication; it was a combination of patience, faith, and unwavering vision.

As the church grew, so did their responsibilities. Volunteers began to rally around the Millers, eager to help with the labor. By 1978, the small wood-framed sanctuary, though expanded multiple times, could no longer accommodate the growing congregation. The time had come for something bigger.

Plans were drawn up for a new five hundred-seat auditorium, complete with office space and a nursery. Sterling purchased an adjacent three-acre tract of land, and in November 1978, construction began. It was a thrilling time, and the excitement among the congregation was palpable. For Sterling and Jean, it was a manifestation of a dream long nurtured and prayed over, one that was now taking physical form.

The new building faced the interstate, becoming a visible testament to the thousands passing through Lafayette. By the summer of 1979, the building had started to take shape, with walls rising and the roof coming together. Sterling, acting as the general contractor, visited the site daily, overseeing every decision, even as he continued his pastoral duties. The Louisiana heat was relentless, but the anticipation of seeing this dream unfold kept him going.

The 2.5-acre dream, which had once been a sixty-dollar venture, was now becoming something far greater. Sterling had learned firsthand that God uses what's in your hand—whether it's sixty dollars, a boat, or a shepherd's rod. Sterling had sixty dollars, Peter had a boat, Moses only a rod. God takes what you have, when yielded to Him, and transforms it. For Sterling, that meant building something tangible out of faith. For others, it could be something else entirely. The principle remained the same: What do you have in your hand? And more importantly, are you willing to give it to God?

WHAT

DO YOU HAVE

IN YOUR HAND?

AND

MORE IMPORTANTLY,

ARE YOU WILLING

TO GIVE IT

TO GOD?

By the summer of 1980, the new building was nearing completion. But on August 18, 1980, tragedy struck. Sterling's only son, Jay, was involved in a serious accident on the job site. What began as a normal day of playing with his sister, Jo Beth, on the construction grounds quickly turned into a life-threatening situation. As Jay ran across the stage that was still under construction, he stepped on a loose board, launching him into the air. He plummeted twelve feet, landing hard on the concrete below across a pile of lumber.

The pain was immediate and severe. Unable to catch his breath, Jay lay in agony as Jo Beth raced to find their father, who was nearby repairing a water line. Sterling rushed to Jay's side, carrying him home to assess the damage. Over the next few hours, Jay's condition worsened. Internal bleeding, high fever, and convulsions set in. By Wednesday, he had lost all feeling in both of his legs and was completely paralyzed from the waist down.

For Sterling and Jean, the weight of the situation was unbearable. The child they had prayed so fervently for, the miracle baby they had never expected to have, now lay still and broken in their living room. Despair settled in as they faced the possibility that their son might never walk again—or worse, might not survive.

Jean stood there, trying to be the rock—the strong pillar of faith and certainty her family needed. Most of all, she tried to be strong for Jay, but no matter how hard she tried, her strength was slipping. Her faith, once so solid, was unraveling with every passing second. Her heart felt as though it was shattering into pieces.

The child she was never supposed to have, the miracle doctors said was impossible, was now fading right before her eyes. The same child she had once held in her arms, overwhelmed with tears of joy, was now cradled in those very same arms. Except this time, the tears were not of joy but of gut-wrenching pain. It wasn't supposed to be this way. Not her baby. Not Jay.

Faith or fear?

Both were there, clawing at her heart and her mind. Both were fighting for control of her soul. In the most excruciating moments of life, these two forces are always present. One whispers hope; the other screams despair. Jean could hear them both so clearly—fear telling her it was over, that she had lost. Faith, though faint, reminded her of the promises spoken so long ago.

Which one would she cling to? Which one would hold her up when everything felt like it was falling apart?

At that moment, in the face of unbearable pain and confusion, Jean held on to the only thing she knew was true. She remembered God's promise—the one He gave her all those years ago, that her children would be mighty upon this earth. The very thought of it was like a lifeline in the middle of a storm.

Fear roared in her ears, but somewhere deep inside, she felt the fragile whisper of faith growing stronger. The God who promised her this miracle child wouldn't abandon her now. No matter how broken her heart felt, no matter how hopeless the situation seemed, Jean believed that the promise she had clung to for so long would now come to pass.

Even as she held Jay in her arms, fighting for his life, she knew—against all the odds, against all the fear—that this was not the end. God's promise wasn't finished yet. A miracle was coming. It had to. And somehow, she would see it.

In that moment of desperation, Sterling sought the Lord, crying out for guidance. He went to his office to get alone and pray. He felt the Lord speak clearly to him: "Lay down tonight next to your son in bed, and the anointing that I have placed in you will transfer to Jay. He will be healed."

With a heart full of faith, Sterling obeyed. I can remember like it was yesterday, my dad telling me those words.

That Thursday night, he carried Jay's frail body to his bed and cradled him throughout the night. The next morning, Jay awoke with his first words: "I'm hungry." It was the first time in over five days that he had expressed a desire to eat. Little by little, his strength began to return.

By Friday evening, Jay felt warmth spreading through his legs. "Dad, come quickly," he called out. "Help me up. I think I can walk."

Sterling hurried to his side and helped him to his feet. With a hand steadying him, Jay took his first steps in days, walking across the room to the kitchen. As he reached his mother, he smiled and said, "Mom, look, I can walk again!"

Within twenty-four hours, the paralysis had vanished, and Jay was running and playing like any nine-year-old boy. The internal bleeding had stopped, his appetite was back, and his strength was fully restored. By Monday morning, Jay was outside, riding the lawnmower as if nothing had ever happened.

That miraculous healing was more than just a personal victory for the Millers; it was a testament to the power of faith and obedience. On November 9, 1980, a day of incredible significance for several reasons, I walked into the new auditorium for the very first time. It was my tenth birthday, the first service in the new building, and a moment that would forever be etched in our family's history.

As I stood on the very stage that had almost taken my life, I held my mother's hand and looked out at the congregation. Jean knelt and whispered words that I would never forget: "Jay, don't ever stop believing because your 'suddenly' is on its way."

Could it be that you are just moments away from your very own "suddenly"—an unexpected breakthrough that changes everything?

Perhaps the painful events you've experienced, the setbacks that have left you feeling broken, are not wasted moments, but pieces of a larger miracle waiting to unfold. What if the heartache you've endured is part of the divine preparation for the next chapter of your life, where the beauty of redemption and restoration takes center stage?

Romans 8:28 assures us that not all things are good, but all things work together for good for those who love God and are called according to His purpose. In God's hands, even our most difficult experiences can become stepping stones toward something far greater than we could imagine. Those trials, the moments that seemed like detours or dead ends, could be the very foundation for a story of triumph, grace, and growth that you will one day look back on with awe.

So, as you stand on the edge of the unknown, remember that the past doesn't define your future—God's purpose does. Every pain, every disappointment, may just be the prelude to the miracle that's on the horizon, where all things truly do work together for your good, in His perfect timing.

AS YOU STAND

ON THE EDGE

OF THE UNKNOWN,

REMEMBER THAT

THE PAST

DOESN'T DEFINE

YOUR FUTURE—

GOD'S PURPOSE

DOES.

CHAPTER 7

FINALLY, A FAMILY!

After eight miscarriages and the trusted word of the doctors in the mid-1960s, Sterling and Jean faced a harsh reality: they would never have biological children of their own. The cost was too high, the risks too dangerous. Another pregnancy would mean putting Jean's life on the line again, and they just couldn't endure another loss. The dream of having a traditional family seemed shattered—an impossible, improbable hope that would require a miracle beyond their control. It was a heartbreaking conclusion, one they had never imagined they'd have to accept.

With heavy hearts, they tried to move forward in their young marriage. They did their best to embrace the memories of each lost child, but the most haunting memory was the burial of their stillborn son, Mathias. His tiny grave felt like a final nail in the coffin of their hopes for a family. His lifeless body had been laid to rest not long ago, and though they were doing their best to press on, the sorrow hung over them like a dark cloud. The dream of a family, of hearing laughter in their home, seemed like a distant fantasy.

Sterling threw himself into his work in the South Louisiana oil fields, but no matter how much he tried to focus, anger and guilt began to consume him. He was furious at the situation—furious at the loss of eight children, and furious at God for allowing it all to happen. Every day, he wrestled with the unbearable thought that he would never extend the Miller family name, never pass it on to the next generation. The legacy he had once dreamed of seemed to evaporate before his eyes. At just thirty-something years old, with so much life ahead of him, Sterling found himself imagining a future without the family he had longed for.

He thought of Jean, of the pain she had endured over those agonizing six years. Eight pregnancies. Eight losses. The emotional scars ran deep, imprinted on their hearts with every baby they buried. There seemed to be no fixing it—no medicine to heal the wounds, no surgery to repair the brokenness. They were trapped in grief with no way out.

And yet, everything would change in the fall of 1965.

Jean's mother, Vivian Hunt, received a phone call from a friend that would alter the course of their lives. The friend's daughter, a young mother of two boys—JoJo, age two, and Henry, age three—was struggling. The biological father was no longer in the picture, and the young mother couldn't provide the care and attention the boys needed. Desperate, she had reached out to her own mother, but the grandmother, already aged and weary, knew she couldn't raise the boys on her own.

That's when the friend thought of Sterling and Jean. She had heard their heartbreaking story of loss and childlessness, and she thought, *Maybe this couple, this young and loving couple, could take in the boys. Maybe they could give them the home they so desperately need.* The friend suggested it to Vivian, who in turn called Sterling and Jean.

The phone call that followed was nothing short of miraculous. Could it really be? After all the heartbreak, all the loss, could they finally have a family? Sterling and Jean's hearts swelled with hope as they began to dream again. The possibilities were almost too much to bear. After six years of sorrow, could two little boys heal their wounds?

The waiting was unbearable. Each day dragged on, and what was merely two weeks felt like two lifetimes. Every minute was filled with anticipation as they made plans, prepared their modest home in Iota, Louisiana, and let themselves dare to dream. Jean and Sterling had waited so long for this moment—years spent praying, hoping, wondering if they would ever be called *Mom* and *Dad*. Now, that dream was close enough to touch, but was it real? Could this truly be happening?

The thought of JoJo and Henry filled every corner of their hearts. They couldn't wait to hold them, to feel the weight of those tiny bodies in their arms, to love them in ways that only parents could. The empty spaces in their home, in their lives, would soon be filled with laughter, with tiny footsteps, and with the sound of their boys' voices calling out, "Mom" and "Dad." They dreamed of all the beautiful firsts: teaching the boys to walk, to talk, to ride bikes down the quiet streets of their little town. They imagined the simple joys of childhood—the wide-eyed wonder of discovery, the carefree days of playing in the yard, the warmth of family dinners together.

For so long, there had been only silence, only darkness, only the ache of unfulfilled hope. But now, light was breaking through—light that flooded their hearts, bursting through every crack with excitement and joy. The pain of waiting, the heartbreak of all the losses, seemed to dim in comparison to the life that was about to unfold before them.

Their hearts raced with a mixture of hope and fear. Could this be the answer to their prayers? Could this really be the fulfillment of their dream? Every moment was filled with breathless anticipation, and every night, they went to bed with visions of JoJo and Henry's little faces, wondering what the future held.

They stood on the brink of something they had longed for their entire lives, and now, that future felt so close, yet still fragile—like a delicate dream that could be snatched away at any moment. And yet, they couldn't help but believe that maybe, just maybe, this was the moment they had been waiting for all along. The long-awaited joy of parenthood, the laughter of children filling their home, the light of love that would forever change their world.

Finally, the day came. In late September 1965, JoJo and Henry arrived at the Miller household, and in an instant, Sterling and Jean were transformed from a grieving couple into a family. They didn't need paperwork or legal processes to feel the depth of this transformation—their hearts had already made the boys their own. Sterling and Jean couldn't believe it. After years of loss, they were now Mom and Dad. It was a dream come true.

The days that followed were filled with memories that would last a lifetime. Sterling taught the boys to ride bikes, to fish, and to play ball in the yard. Jean made sure they were fed and clothed and—most importantly—taught them to pray. Though Jean had drifted from her faith over the years, this newfound motherhood began to rekindle something inside her. The promise she had made as a young girl—to raise her children to know and love God—was reignited.

AFTER YEARS

OF LOSS,

THEY WERE

NOW

MOM AND DAD.

IT WAS A

DREAM

COME TRUE.

But there was tension. Sterling's anger toward God had only grown over the years. His bitterness ran deep, and though Jean quietly took JoJo and Henry to church every Sunday, she knew this might cause friction. Every week, Jean's faith was slowly resurrecting, little by little, as she prayed with her sons and guided them in the ways of the Lord. Sterling remained distant, refusing to join them.

And yet, JoJo and Henry were learning to pray. Each night, before supper, one of the boys would bow their heads and say, "God, thank You for this food. Thank You for our wonderful family. Thank You for my mom and dad. Lord, please help my daddy come to church with us. Amen."

It was an innocent prayer, but one that stirred deep emotions. Jean would later laugh with her children, JoBeth and Jay, about the awkwardness of those moments, recalling how Sterling would grow angry, though never at the boys—always at her. Yet the prayers continued, night after night.

But then, in late October 1967, a phone call came that shattered their hearts into pieces once more. It was the kind of call that seemed impossible, a nightmare in the middle of their waking life. On the other end of the line were the biological parents of JoJo and Henry—their voices steady, but the message devastating. After years of being apart, they had reunited, and now, they wanted their children back.

The shock was immediate, a gut-punch that left Sterling and Jean gasping for air. The pain gripped them like a vice, the disbelief clouding their minds. *How could this be happening?* After all this time, after the love and care they had poured into these boys, after building a life together—*their* life—how could it all be taken away in a moment? They had dreamed of a future with JoJo and Henry, a future that now seemed to be slipping through their fingers, like sand they couldn't hold on to no matter how tightly they clenched their fists.

Desperation set in. Could they fight it? Could they appeal to the courts, make a case for the life they had built, for the love they had shared? The questions flew out faster than they could think. But even as they asked, somewhere deep down, they knew the truth. The law was not on their side. There was no recourse, no loophole, no way to hold on to the family they had prayed so long to have. JoJo and Henry were not just slipping away—they were being torn from their arms, from their hearts, from the home they had built.

The days that followed were a blur of grief and helplessness.

Sterling and Jean were summoned to court in October 1967, where their fate—and the fate of their family—would be sealed. As they walked into that courthouse, the weight of loss pressed heavily on their shoulders. They were no strangers to loss, but this—this was a wound that cut deeper than anything they had faced before.

How do you prepare to say goodbye to the children who have become your heart? How do you let go of the ones you had dreamed would call you "Mom" and "Dad" forever? As they stood before the judge, time seemed to hang in a fragile balance. Every word spoken felt like a thread pulling, threatening to unravel everything they held dear. The final decision had not yet been made, but the weight of uncertainty pressed heavily on Sterling and Jean's hearts.

They carried not just the ache of what might come but the unbearable tension of hope colliding with fear. They had given their hearts fully to JoJo and Henry, and now those hearts hung in the balance, teetering between love and loss. Their home, once filled with laughter and joy, seemed suspended in a cruel limbo, waiting for news that could either restore or shatter their dreams.

The pain of not knowing cut deeply, a kind of sorrow that left them breathless and unsure of how to move forward. This was a pain they had never imagined, the kind that leaves you breathless, unsure of how to move forward.

When life feels like it's slipping through your grasp, when control seems distant, and you feel overwhelmed by uncertainty, take heart—God is holding you even when everything else feels unsteady. Psalm 46:10 gently reminds us, "Be still, and know that I am God." In the moments when life feels chaotic or beyond your control, He is still sovereign, still present, and still faithful.

In those times when it feels like you're losing your grip, God invites you to release your worries into His hands. Jesus said in Matthew 11:28, "Come to me, all you who are weary and burdened, and I will give you rest." It's in surrender, not striving, that we find peace. Let go of the weight you've been carrying—your fears, your uncertainties—and trust that God is in control, even when everything else seems out of reach.

Isaiah 41:10 promises that God will strengthen you and uphold you with His righteous right hand. You are never out of His grasp, and He will not let you fall. What may feel like slipping to you is God positioning you for something greater, something beyond your understanding right now. His ways are higher than ours, and He knows the plans He has for you—plans to prosper you and give you hope and a future (Jeremiah 29:11).

Remember, you don't have to have it all together or figure everything out. Simply trust that the One who created the universe also holds your life in His hands. He is faithful, and He will guide you through this season, offering peace, strength, and clarity in His time. Keep holding onto Him, for He will never let go of you.

CHAPTER 8

"YOU HAVE THIRTY DAYS"

S terling and Jean walked into the courtroom in Jennings, Louisiana, in late October 1967, gripping JoJo and Henry's tiny hands, their hearts heavy with a looming dread. The boys, just four and five, were too young to understand the weight of the situation unfolding around them. To them, it was just another day with their mom and dad, who kept reassuring them with whispers of, "It's going to be okay." But as they approached the heavy courtroom doors, Sterling and Jean could feel the future they had built with these two boys slipping away with every step. Their hands, once comforting, now clenched tighter as if holding on could stop the inevitable.

Sitting in the cold, sterile courtroom, they tried to keep the boys entertained, forcing smiles as they recalled the simple joys of the past two years. They had taught JoJo and Henry to speak their first words, count to ten, and sing the alphabet. They remembered the nights gathered around the fire pit, roasting marshmallows, and the way JoJo would accidentally push Henry too hard on the swing set, sending him flying and causing fits of giggles. Jean always dressed them like twins, even though Henry— ever the proud older brother—made sure JoJo knew who was in charge. In those moments of waiting, they tried to hold onto the laughter, the fleeting innocence of childhood, as if that could somehow freeze time.

But then the door swung open, and the judge walked in, taking his seat at the bench. The weight of the moment fell like a lead blanket. The room fell into an oppressive silence as the deputy announced that court was in session. Sterling and Jean, seated on one side of the room with JoJo and Henry between them, could feel the tension rise. On the opposite side, the biological parents sat quietly, accompanied by their own family. The stark division between them felt like a chasm, separating not just two sets of parents, but two possible futures.

The judge listened to both stories for hours, carefully considering each side. Sterling and Jean's story was one of love—a deep, unbreakable love that had transformed these boys' lives. When JoJo and Henry arrived on their doorstep, they had been scared, carrying only the clothes on their backs. But within two years, they had become a family. Sterling and Jean had given them not just a home, but a life filled with warmth, care, and stability. They had created memories that most families build over decades—teaching the boys how to ride bikes, say prayers, and play catch. They had stitched together a life from the fragments of brokenness the boys had arrived with.

The biological parents, on the other hand, pleaded their case, expressing regret for the past but claiming they were now ready to reunite with their children. They had made mistakes but felt it was time to take their boys back and make amends. The judge, conflicted, recognized the strength of the biological bond but was equally moved by the love Sterling and Jean had shown.

Then, in a move that stunned the courtroom, the judge called the boys up to his bench. Looking into their young, innocent eyes, he asked, "Go stand by your mom and dad." For a moment, the entire courtroom seemed to hold its breath, waiting for what felt like a lifetime in those few seconds. Without hesitation, both JoJo and Henry ran straight into the arms of Sterling and Jean, their cries breaking the silence. "Mama, don't let them take us!" JoJo sobbed. "Daddy, please, we don't want to go!" Henry echoed through his tears. Their small arms clung tightly around their parents' necks, refusing to let go.

There wasn't a dry eye in the courtroom. The tension, the heartbreak—it was unbearable. Sterling and Jean, their hearts shattered, held their boys as if it would be the last time. The judge, visibly torn, called for a ten-minute recess to gather his thoughts. Those ten minutes felt like an eternity. Sterling and Jean sat in silence, the weight of their grief pressing down on them. Their minds raced through the memories—of the miscarriages, the stillborn baby, Mathias, and all the heartache they thought they had left behind. But JoJo and Henry had healed those wounds. These boys had brought them back to life and restored their hope.

As the judge returned, the courtroom once again fell silent. Sterling and Jean braced themselves for the verdict, knowing that whatever came next would change everything. The judge's voice, steady but filled with regret, finally delivered the crushing blow.

"Sterling and Jean Miller, you have thirty days to prepare the children to return to their biological parents."

The gavel dropped with a resounding thud, and in that instant, the world as they knew it shattered. The echo of the judge's decision reverberated in their hearts, a final, unrelenting blow that stole the breath from their lungs. Thirty days. Just thirty days to say goodbye to the life they had dreamed of. Thirty days to watch everything they had hoped for slip away like a fading memory.

For so long, they had imagined a lifetime with JoJo and Henry—a future filled with laughter, scraped knees, bedtime stories, and the simple joys of watching their boys grow. But now, that dream had been condensed into the cruel reality of a single month. Thirty short days to pack away a lifetime of hopes and say farewell to the sons they had already claimed in their hearts.

As they left the courtroom, the weight of the moment pressed down on them like a suffocating blanket. The boys' small hands were still tightly wrapped in theirs as if holding on to the only security they had ever known. Jean and Sterling exchanged a glance, their eyes brimming with unshed tears, but in that look was a silent resolve—*we will make every moment count.*

Each day became a precious gift, a bittersweet countdown to an inevitable goodbye. Every laugh, every shared meal, every quiet moment at home took on a deeper significance. They played in the yard until the sun set, cooked their favorite meals, and told them stories by the fire. Every moment, every smile, was savored like it might be the last.

And yet, beneath the surface of their brave faces, a storm raged in their hearts. How do you fit a lifetime of love into thirty days? How do you teach them everything they'll need to know when you know that time is slipping away with each passing hour? How do you say goodbye to the boys who have become your world?

The countdown to farewell was unbearable, but in those final thirty days, Jean and Sterling poured out every ounce of love they had, creating memories that would linger long after the boys had gone. They had dreamed of a lifetime together, but now, all they had was thirty days—and they were determined to fill those days with a love that would last forever.

For the next thirty days, they created as many memories as they could. Every meal was shared together, every bike ride cherished. They took long walks, told stories, laughed until their sides ached, and, on weekends, drove to Crowley for ice cream. Sterling and Jean didn't let a single moment slip away without savoring it. But as the days dwindled, the looming goodbye became harder to bear.

The last three days were the hardest. They packed the boys' clothes, their toys, their crayons, baseball gloves, and bicycles. But those final hours weren't spent outdoors or on adventures. They stayed inside, on the living room floor, building puzzles, sharing quiet conversations, and holding each other. Sterling and Jean soaked in every detail—the way JoJo's curls bounced when he laughed, how Henry's serious expression would break into a mischievous grin.

Jean, in the quiet moments, wrote down everything in her journal. She recounted the day JoJo and Henry had first arrived, the memories they had built, and how much these boys had healed their broken hearts. As she wrote, tears fell, blurring the ink, but she kept writing—because this was the only way to keep them with her, to hold onto the pieces of the family she was about to lose.

HIS ARMS

ARE WIDE OPEN,

READY TO CATCH

EVERY FRAGMENT

OF YOUR PAIN

AND TURN IT

INTO SOMETHING

BEAUTIFUL.

On the thirtieth day, a car pulled up the driveway, and they knew what it meant. JoJo and Henry's suitcases were packed, their little red wagon filled with toys waiting by the door. Sterling held Henry, and Jean held JoJo, their hearts breaking all over again as they approached the car. The boys, sensing what was about to happen, clung tighter, their little arms wrapped around their parents' necks. "No, Mama, no! Daddy, please! We want to stay here!" Their cries were gut-wrenching, their sobs echoing in the stillness of the morning.

With trembling hands and hearts shattered beyond repair, Sterling and Jean gently pried the boys from their arms and handed them over. As the car pulled away, taking not just the boys but their dreams, their future, and their very hearts with it, they stood there, watching until the car disappeared from view. All that remained were a few photographs, two years of memories, and a pain so deep it felt as if it would never heal.

When your heart is broken, it can feel as though the pieces are too shattered to ever come together again. The pain may be overwhelming, but in the midst of your hurt, remember that God is near to the brokenhearted. Psalm 34:18 reminds us that the Lord is close to those who are crushed in spirit, and He binds up their wounds.

Healing from a broken heart is never an instant process. It can feel like an unending journey, as though the weight of sorrow may never lift. But with God, healing is a sure promise. He knows your pain intimately, sees every tear, and feels the depths of your grief. He doesn't just stand by and watch—He enters into your pain, holding you with a tenderness that only He can give. His Word promises that He will bring beauty from ashes (Isaiah 61:3) and turn your mourning into joy (Jeremiah 31:13). Even when your heart feels shattered beyond repair, God is working in ways you cannot yet see, shaping and restoring you, weaving together every broken piece for your good (Romans 8:28).

If you are in a season of heartache, lean into His presence like never before. Cry out to Him, for He listens to every word, even the ones you can't find the strength to say aloud. Pour out your heart in prayer, knowing that He is near to the brokenhearted and binds up their wounds (Psalm 147:3). His arms are wide open, ready to catch every fragment of your pain and turn it into something beautiful. Let His Word surround you like a shield, filling your mind and soul with the comfort of His promises. These aren't empty words—they are living, breathing promises from a God who never fails.

Understand this: your heart is safe in His hands. He is the master Healer, the One who can restore what seems irreparable. The process may be slow, but His faithfulness never wavers. He will rebuild you, piece by piece, with a care and love that far sur- passes anything you could imagine. Trust that as you surrender your pain to Him, He will strengthen and renew you. What you see as broken, He sees as an opportunity for redemption. What you think is lost forever, He will restore in ways more magnificent than you ever dreamed.

Healing will come, even if it feels slow. God is faithful, and He will make all things new in His perfect time. Hold on to hope, for there is healing in His love. His plans for you are good, filled with peace and a future brighter than you can comprehend (Jer- emiah 29:11). Don't rush the process—trust that each day, God is writing a new chapter for your life—one that is filled with redemption, restoration, and grace.

Take it one step at a time, knowing that even in your pain, God is there, shaping you, molding you, and preparing you for the blessings yet to come. Healing may not be instant, but it is certain. Trust the One who holds your future, for He is turning your mourning into dancing, and your tears into joy. Hold fast to the truth that God's love for you is unwavering, and He will carry you through this season into something far more beautiful than you could ever imagine.

CHAPTER 9

NO ONE BUT JESUS

As the car disappeared down the road, the dust hung in the air, lingering like the shattered dreams Sterling and Jean had been forced to leave behind. The vehicle, carrying JoJo and Henry away, had vanished from sight, but the ache of what could have been remained, hanging over them like a heavy, suffocating cloud.

The walk back to their tiny two-bedroom home was filled with a silence so thick it was almost unbearable. This house, which had once echoed with the laughter and chatter of the boys, now felt painfully empty. The absence of their toys, clothes, and belongings was obvious, but the emptiness that weighed on Sterling and Jean's hearts was far more profound. It felt as though their future had driven away with that car, their hope as clouded as the dust that had been kicked up.

When they stepped into the living room, Brother Kenneth Wall, the pastor of the small Baptist church that Jean and the boys had faithfully attended, was waiting for them. This was the same church where the boys had prayed—week after week—that their daddy would join them. But Sterling never did. He had stayed away, his heart hardened by the years of loss and pain that had shaped his life. Each miscarriage, each heartache, each unanswered prayer had added another brick to the wall he had built between himself and God. And now, with the boys gone, surely his bitterness would deepen.

But today, something was different.

As Brother Wall entered the room, Sterling's resolve broke. The man who had survived the war in Vietnam, who had stood strong through unimaginable loss, couldn't hold on any longer. His heart, already bruised and battered, had been pushed beyond its limit. The anger that had kept him going, the bitterness that had fueled him for so long, now felt hollow and weak in the face of this overwhelming grief.

Sterling, the man who had always prided himself on his strength—six feet one inch, 230 pounds, tough as steel—collapsed. Tears, raw and uncontrollable, poured from his eyes. His shoulders shook as sob after sob escaped him. The strength he had always relied on had finally failed him. His mind was flooded with images of JoJo and Henry being torn from his arms, their fingernails digging into his neck as they clung to him. The physical pain was nothing compared to the emotional agony he felt now.

He had witnessed death before—he had seen the horrors of Vietnam, where life could be snuffed out in an instant. He had stood by helplessly as his sister was tragically taken in a car accident. But nothing—*nothing*—could have prepared Sterling for the gut-wrenching heartache of losing his sons. This pain was different. It was deeper, more raw, a kind of suffering that tore at his very soul. It was as though the weight of the world had been dropped onto his shoulders, crushing him until he could no longer stand beneath it. Every breath felt heavy, every moment like an eternity of grief. He had lost more than his sons; he had lost his hope.

Sterling's heart, once so full of dreams for his family, was now shattered into pieces too broken to pick up. The pain was unbearable, a dark void that consumed him from the inside out. And though he had endured so much in his life, this loss left him feeling utterly hollow, drained of the strength to carry on. How could anyone survive this? How could anyone heal from such devastation?

It was in the depths of this despair, when the silence in the house was too loud to bear, that Brother Wall entered. He had been a friend, a man of God, and someone who could see the brokenness in Sterling's eyes. Without saying much, Brother Wall placed a hand on Sterling's trembling shoulder and, with a voice soft but full of conviction, said, "Sterling, there's only One who can heal your broken heart, and His name is Jesus."

Those words hung in the air, gentle yet powerful. Sterling had heard about Jesus before, but at this moment, those words cut through his pain like a beam of light breaking through a stormy sky. For the first time in years, Sterling felt something shift. The weight of the grief, the bitterness, the years of anger—it all came to the surface, raw and exposed.

At that moment, in the stillness of their living room, something broke inside him. Sterling collapsed to his knees as if the earth beneath him could no longer support the burden he carried. His body shook with sobs that he could no longer hold back. It was as if the dam of his emotions, held back for so long, had finally given way. The grief, the pain, the anger—all of it spilled out.

FOR THE

FIRST TIME

IN YEARS,

STERLING

FELT SOMETHING

SHIFT.

With trembling hands lifted toward heaven and tears streaming down his face, Sterling cried out from the deepest part of his soul, "Jesus, help me. Jesus, heal me. If You're real, heal my broken heart."

It wasn't a polished prayer. It wasn't filled with theological words or rehearsed lines. It was raw, desperate, and unfiltered. But in that moment, it was the truest thing Sterling had ever said. He had nothing left to offer but his brokenness, and he laid it all before Jesus.

And in that moment, something miraculous happened. It wasn't loud or dramatic, but it was real. Sterling felt the first stirrings of peace in a heart that had been ravaged by loss. The weight that had been crushing him didn't disappear entirely, but it began to lift, piece by piece. He could feel the presence of something—*someone*—greater than his pain, greater than his sorrow, wrapping around him like a warm embrace.

For the first time in a long time, he felt hope.

As Sterling knelt on the floor, tears falling freely, he knew deep within his soul that Jesus had heard him. That the God he had cried out to had responded. Healing wouldn't come all at once, but in that moment, a seed of restoration was planted, and though Sterling didn't have all the answers, he knew one thing: Jesus was real, and He had begun to heal his broken heart. The journey ahead would still be difficult, but he would no longer walk it alone.

It was a desperate plea, a cry from a man who had reached the end of himself. And in that moment, something miraculous happened. In the quiet of that small house in Iota, Louisiana, Sterling Miller met Jesus. Brother Wall led him through the prayer of salvation, and as Sterling repeated the words, something deep inside him shifted. The bitterness that had once consumed him began to lift, replaced by an unfamiliar peace.

Jean, who had been in the next room, entered the living room just in time to witness the transformation. Sterling, the man who had resisted God for so long, had finally surrendered. The man who had refused to set foot in a church, who had rejected his children's prayers, was now kneeling in repentance, his heart laid bare before the Lord.

It was a moment Jean would never forget—a moment that marked the beginning of a new chapter in their lives.

The change in Sterling was almost immediate. In the days that followed, the transformation was undeniable. His mind, once clouded by anger and bitterness, was now clear. His heart, once hardened by years of pain, was softened. His faith, which had been non-existent, suddenly became alive. There was a new hunger in him—a desire to know more about the God who had healed his broken heart. He found himself devouring the Bible, a book he had once dismissed as irrelevant. Every word seemed to leap off the page, filling the emptiness in his soul.

As he returned to work in the oil fields, Sterling couldn't shake the feeling that something had changed. The job, which had once been his pride and his livelihood, now felt hollow. He felt a stirring deep inside him, a call that he couldn't ignore. His passions, his dreams, his desires—they were all shifting.

And then, just two weeks after that life-changing moment in the living room, Sterling felt an unmistakable call to ministry. It was a call that surprised even him. The man who had never cared for church, who had never owned a Bible, was now feeling led to become a pastor. It was a calling that could only have come from God.

Sterling shared his newfound dream with Jean, and together, they began researching seminaries. After some searching, they discovered Dallas Theological Seminary, and without hesitation, they knew that was where they were meant to be.

With no job lined up, no promise of acceptance into the seminary, and no family waiting for them in Texas, Sterling and Jean packed up everything they owned into their 1966 Chevy wagon. It was a leap of faith, a bold step into the unknown, but Sterling knew that God had a plan for them.

In late August of 1968, they set out for Dallas, Texas. It was the beginning of a new life—a life filled with hope, dreams, and a purpose that only God could give. As they drove away from the home they had known for so long, Sterling reflected on how much had changed in such a short amount of time. The man he had been—the bitter, angry, wounded man—was gone. In his place stood a man filled with hope, a man who had finally found healing in the arms of Jesus.

Nothing but Jesus could have transformed Sterling Miller. Nothing but His grace could have healed the wounds that had once seemed impossible to overcome.

As they drove toward Dallas, Sterling knew one thing for certain: he was no longer the same man. The future, once clouded with uncertainty and pain, now stretched before him, bright and filled with the promise of new beginnings. With Jesus leading the way, Sterling dared to trust God, knowing that his life, his dreams, and his heart were now in the hands of the One who could heal all things.

Taking a step of faith into the unknown can feel daunting, even overwhelming. But it is in these moments of uncertainty that God calls us to trust Him more deeply. Hebrews 11:1 (ESV) reminds us, "Faith is the assurance of things hoped for, the conviction of things not seen." Though the path ahead may be unclear, know that God is already there, preparing the way.

Throughout Scripture, we see examples of ordinary people who took bold steps of faith, not because they knew every detail of the journey but because they trusted the One who called them. Abraham left his homeland without knowing where he was going, but he followed God's promise. Peter stepped out of the boat onto the water, not because the waves were calm but because Jesus was calling him.

God often leads us into the unknown so that our faith can grow. Proverbs 3:5-6 encourages us to "Trust in the LORD with all your heart and lean not on your own understanding; in all your ways submit to him, and he will make your paths straight." When you step forward in faith, even without all the answers, you are choosing to trust God's wisdom and His perfect timing. He sees what you cannot, and He is working all things for your good (Romans 8:28).

Though the road ahead may be unfamiliar, God's promises are your firm foundation. He will guide you, strengthen you, and provide for you along the way. Remember, God is not asking you to walk this journey alone—He is walking with you. His Word is a lamp to your feet and a light to your path (Psalm 119:105), illuminating each step, even when you cannot see the whole road.

THOUGH THE

PATH AHEAD

MAY BE UNCLEAR,

KNOW THAT

GOD IS

ALREADY THERE,

PREPARING

THE WAY.

So, take that step of faith with confidence. The same God who parted the seas and calmed the storms is holding your future. And as you step out in faith, He will meet you there, leading you into new blessings, growth, and purpose that are far beyond what you could imagine. Trust in His faithfulness, for He will never leave you nor forsake you (Deuteronomy 31:6).

CHAPTER 10

WORK YOUR DREAM

On February 10, 1973, a peculiar opportunity arose in Kaplan, Louisiana. A local dentist, preparing for a new brick-and-mortar office, needed to clear an aging 24x60-foot structure off his land. Word of this surplus building traveled to Sterling Miller—a man with a dream, 2.5 acres of land, but no building to hold his vision. The timing felt almost too good to be true.

Without delay, Sterling turned to Jean. "Let's go see it," he said. Together, they climbed into his old Dodge pickup and headed south, unsure of what they would find but certain that God had something in store. When they arrived, their hearts sank at the sight. The building was an eyesore—over thirty years old, its wooden exterior rotted, windows shattered, and paint peeling like a forgotten relic of the past.

But Sterling and Jean were not discouraged. As they walked around the crumbling office, hand in hand, they looked past the decay. They saw potential. Where others might have seen a decaying husk, they envisioned a sanctuary. "There's the stage," Sterling said, pointing to a storage area. "And that's where the front door will go," Jean added, her eyes lighting up. Where narrow office walls stood, they saw an auditorium—a space big enough to seat over a hundred people, even though their congregation currently numbered just four: Sterling, Jean, and their two small children, JoBeth and Jay.

The building was theirs for the taking as long as they could move it. Sterling sprang into action, calling every contact he had. Eventually, he found a mover out of Crowley, Louisiana, willing to transport the building those thirty-three miles to 223 Stone Avenue for $300. But there was a catch: the building had to pass beneath a newly constructed interstate, and to make the journey, the roof would need to be cut off, flipped upside down, and placed inside the structure. It was a risk—a gamble—but they knew this building was the key to bringing their dream to life.

The real work began as soon as the building arrived on Stone Avenue. The structure was barely functional. Water, sewer, and electrical lines all needed to be installed. The interior had to be gutted and rebuilt. But Sterling wasn't one to shy away from a challenge. Day after day, he labored with his own hands. He knocked down walls, hammered new beams into place, rewired rooms, and painted every surface. There were days when the work seemed endless, when he would arrive early in the morning with a shovel and a bucket, prepared to empty the septic tank himself just to ensure the workers had a working facility.

While Sterling handled the physical labor, Jean was equally hard at work. She nurtured the community, praying and encouraging the small group of believers who had begun to gather. People like Grace and Willie Klump and Travis and Wanda Hardy became fixtures in those early days. They weren't just building a church—they were building a family—one relationship, one act of faith at a time.

Yet doubt hung thick in the air, like a shadow that wouldn't leave. People walked by the run-down dentist's office, shaking their heads in disbelief, wondering how anyone could see potential in such a broken, forgotten building. The peeling paint, cracked windows, and overgrown weeds didn't speak of hope or promise—they spoke of abandonment. Few could fathom how this weary structure could ever become a beacon of life, and even fewer believed that Sterling and Jean, with their modest resources and unassuming presence, could transform this wreck into a thriving church, let alone establish a Christian school that would impact generations.

Could they really do it? Was this just a misguided dream? But Sterling and Jean didn't just have a dream—they had a conviction that went deeper than anyone else's doubt. Where others saw decay and failure, they saw a foundation waiting to be built upon, a canvas that God Himself had handed them. This wasn't just about restoring a building. It was about planting seeds of faith that would grow into something far greater than the eye could see.

Sterling and Jean had learned something that not everyone understood: while prayer is the bedrock of every dream, faith without action is like a fire without fuel. They knew that God would move, but they also knew He expected them to move first. You pray like it's all up to God, but you work like it's all up to you.

WHILE PRAYER

IS THE

BEDROCK OF

EVERY DREAM,

FAITH

WITHOUT ACTION

IS LIKE

A FIRE

WITHOUT FUEL.

So, with relentless faith and calloused hands, they rolled up their sleeves and got to work. Every day, they prayed, not with timid hope, but with bold expectation. They prayed for provision, for strength, for miracles. But they didn't stop at prayer. They poured everything they had—heart, soul, sweat, and tears—into making the dream a reality. They hammered nails, swept floors, and scrubbed walls. They knocked on doors, made phone calls, and shared their vision with anyone who would listen. Every hour spent in prayer was matched by an hour of labor, for they understood that faith in action was the bridge between the dream and its fulfillment.

The process was slow, painfully slow at times. There were days when the weight of doubt pressed in on them, when the voices of disbelief seemed louder than their own prayers. But in those moments, they clung to the conviction that God had placed this dream in their hearts for a reason, and they wouldn't stop until it became a reality.

With each brushstroke of fresh paint, with each piece of debris cleared away, they weren't just renovating a building—they were laying the foundation of a vision that stretched far beyond brick and mortar. They were building a place where faith could thrive, where lives would be transformed, and where children would grow up learning about the God who makes all things possible.

Slowly but surely, the vision began to take shape. The walls of that old dentist's office started to reflect the hope Sterling and Jean had always seen in their hearts. The echoes of doubt were replaced by the sounds of hammering, singing, and the voices of people coming together to support what once seemed impossible.

They knew that what they were building wasn't just for them—it was for the generations to come, for the lives that would be changed in that very place—and while many had doubted, Sterling and Jean had no doubt that with God, they could accomplish what others called impossible. Their faith was not blind; it was bold. Their dream wasn't just a vision—it was a promise from God that, with enough faith and hard work, He would take the smallest seed of hope and grow it into something extraordinary.

That old building, once written off by so many, became a monument to the power of faith and determination. A church was born. A school was established. And the dream Sterling and Jean carried in their hearts became a living testament to what God can do when you pray like it's all up to Him and work like it's all up to you.

Even JoBeth and Jay, their toddlers, joined the effort. They could be seen carrying small tools, sweeping debris from the floors, and proudly helping wherever they could. This was more than a building project; it was a family mission.

From the very beginning, the ministry was anchored on 1 Corinthians 1:7 (NKJV), "So that you come short in no gift, eagerly waiting for the revelation of our Lord Jesus Christ." God had planted that verse in Sterling's heart years before in Dallas, a reminder that if they trusted Him, every need would be met. Time and again, this promise came to life. When they needed a building, it appeared. When they needed workers, they showed up. When they needed a miracle, God delivered.

But it wasn't easy. Some days, the weight of the dream felt overwhelming. It was hard to be patient, hard to wait on God's timing. There were moments of doubt when the obstacles seemed insurmountable. Yet, just as doubt began to creep in, God would send exactly what they needed—whether it was a person, a resource, or a word of encouragement. Sterling and Jean learned that God's timing is always perfect, even when the waiting is painful.

God has placed a dream inside of you—a vision uniquely designed for you to carry out in this world. But having a dream isn't the end of the journey; it's only the beginning. God calls us to not just believe in His promises but to actively pursue them, to take the dream He's given us and work with our hands to bring it to life.

In Ecclesiastes 9:10, the Word encourages us, "Whatever your hand finds to do, do it with all your might." That dream in your heart will not grow on its own. It requires effort, dedication, and hard work. But here's the beauty: when you step out in faith and begin to labor over the vision God has entrusted to you, He meets you in that place of work. He takes your efforts, no matter how small, and multiplies them in ways you cannot imagine.

Just like a farmer must plant seeds, water them, and tend the soil, you must invest in the dream God has given you. The sweat, the perseverance, and the diligence of your hands are all part of the process. Proverbs 14:23 reminds us, "All hard work brings a profit, but mere talk leads only to poverty." Talking about the dream, wishing it into existence, will never bring it to life. It is the work of your hands, partnered with the strength of the Lord, that will transform the dream into reality.

IT IS THE WORK

OF YOUR HANDS,

PARTNERED

WITH THE STRENGTH

OF THE LORD,

THAT WILL TRANSFORM

THE DREAM

INTO REALITY.

Do not be discouraged when the road is difficult or when the progress seems slow. Remember, even when we cannot see it, God is always working behind the scenes. Galatians 6:9 encourages us, "Let us not become weary in doing good, for at the proper time we will reap a harvest if we do not give up." Every step of obedience, every task completed, is part of God's divine plan for your life.

God has not called you to do this alone. His Spirit empowers you for the work ahead. As you work, trust that He will provide the strength, the wisdom, and the resources you need. Commit your plans to the Lord, as Proverbs 16:3 says, and He will establish your steps.

So, work the dream God has placed inside of you. With every effort, with every swing of the hammer, every idea brought to life, you are honoring the Lord. He sees your labor, He hears your prayers, and in His perfect timing, the harvest will come. Keep your hands steady, your faith strong, and your eyes fixed on Him. The dream will come to pass, and it will be greater than you ever imagined.

After ten long, grueling weeks of sweat and tears, the transformation was finally complete. The building that had once been an old, rundown office was now a place of worship. The walls had been rebuilt, the paint freshly applied, and gravel spread to create a parking lot. Wooden benches were brought in for seating, and the place was ready for its first service.

The date was set for April 22, 1973. Not only was it the official opening of TFC, but it was also Easter Sunday. As the congregation gathered that morning, the air buzzed with excitement. They were celebrating more than the resurrection of Christ; they were celebrating the resurrection of a dream—a dream that had been buried under layers of doubt, hard work, and faith. As Sterling and Jean stood in that remodeled building, surrounded by their growing church family, they knew this was only the beginning. The dream that had started on 2.5 acres of land was alive, and God was just getting started.

CHAPTER 11

MY TWO MIRACLE BABIES

In the summer of 1968, Sterling and Jean Miller packed up their modest station wagon and began a new journey, leaving behind the familiar sights of Iota, Louisiana, and heading toward Dallas, Texas. The silence in the car was heavy with anticipation—new dreams, new challenges, and new faith lay ahead. For years, their hearts had been battered by loss, pain, and disappointment. But God, in His mercy, had begun the process of healing their deepest wounds. Now, with renewed hearts and unwavering hope, they drove forward into the unknown, trusting that this new season was a divine appointment.

The 384-mile drive may have taken eight hours, but for Sterling and Jean, it was a lifetime in the making. With their suitcases packed and a well-worn Bible resting between them, they felt that they had everything they needed. Faith to face the unknown, trust in a God who had radically changed the heart of an oil field worker, and the belief that their future was pregnant with divine possibilities. As they left behind the sorrows of the past, they stepped into a season of faith, obedience, and trust.

September 3, 1968, was the first day of classes for Sterling at the theological seminary. It was also Jean's first day working at a bank, just a three-minute walk from their tiny one-bedroom apartment. By divine design, they had found the apartment, the job, and Sterling's place at the seminary all in one phone call. The landlord happened to be the bank manager, who just happened to need a secretary. The pieces fell into place as if heaven itself had arranged their path.

Sterling and Jean knew this was no coincidence. This was a divine calling, a purpose orchestrated by God. They were young, eager, and willing to learn. They knew that one day, they would become pastors, shepherding others in their faith, but for now, they were students in every sense—learning, growing, and trusting God to lead them in His time.

By December 1968, just three months into their new life, the Millers were already envisioning the future. They prayed daily, asking God for guidance. One morning, in a quiet moment, Sterling asked Jean a question that had been stirring in his heart, a question that weighed heavy on his spirit. "Jean, if we're going to be pastors and families come to us for guidance, how can we teach them to raise a family when we don't have one ourselves? That dream feels dead."

Jean, ever the beacon of faith, looked at Sterling with tears in her eyes and said, "Sterling, I don't know how or when, but I believe God has a plan. Even in the brokenness, I trust that His plan is good."

But the question lingered in Sterling's mind, refusing to fade. It gnawed at him as days turned into weeks. How could they pastor families without children of their own? He wrestled with God in prayer, seeking an answer. And then, like a sunrise breaking through the night, God spoke. The words of 1 Corinthians 1:7

echoed in his heart: "So that you come short in no gift, eagerly while waiting for the revelation of our Lord Jesus Christ" (NKJV).

God instructed Sterling and Jean to cling to that verse, to hold it close, and never let it slip from their hearts. The message was clear: Whatever you need, when you need it, it will be there. Stirred by this revelation, Sterling wrote the words down, and with newfound boldness, he brought his deepest longing before the Lord. "God," he prayed, "if we are to pastor families, we will need a family of our own. We're asking for one child. Just one, Lord."

They knew the risks. They knew what the doctors had said about Jean's health after enduring eight devastating miscarriages. But this time, they didn't lean on medical reports or fear. They placed their hope squarely in God's hands.

And then, it happened. Just weeks after Sterling's desperate, heartfelt prayer, the news came. It was the kind of news that made time stand still, where the world seemed to hold its breath in anticipation. Jean was pregnant—for the ninth time. The words echoed in their hearts, filling the quiet spaces of their home with fragile hope, a flicker of light in the darkness that had surrounded them for so long.

But even as hope began to swell, it was accompanied by the weight of their past. This wasn't their first time receiving this kind of news. Eight times before, they had felt this same spark of hope, only to have it cruelly extinguished by loss. The memories of their previous heartbreaks were still fresh, the scars deep, as if etched into their very souls. They had been here before—full of dreams and expectations, only to have those dreams collapse into sorrow.

Still, something felt different this time. Was it the power of the prayer Sterling had prayed? Was it the fact that they had surrendered it all to God, trusting Him in a way they never had before? There was a new sense of possibility, though it was fragile, as delicate as a flame flickering in the wind. Could this be the child they had longed for? Could this be the baby that would finally make their long-held dream of a family come true?

Every day was a balancing act between faith and fear. They dared to dream, dared to envision holding this child in their arms, but with every step forward, they were cautious, guarding their hearts against the pain they had known too well. Jean's hand would rest on her growing belly, and a quiet prayer would escape her lips, "Lord, let this be the one."

Sterling, too, prayed with renewed fervor, asking God to protect this new life, to guard the baby growing within Jean. He would lay his hands on her belly each night, as they whispered prayers together, standing in faith while knowing the fragility of the journey ahead. Could they trust again after so much loss? Could they open their hearts to hope, knowing the devastation that could follow?

With every day that passed, hope grew a little stronger. They clung to it, but not blindly—this was hope forged in the fire of their past trials, a hope that had been refined through tears and suffering. They knew they couldn't control the outcome, but they could trust the One who held their future in His hands. And so, they chose to hope, step by step, day by day.

In the quiet moments, they would whisper to each other, daring to believe that maybe—just maybe—this time would be different. They imagined the sound of tiny footsteps in their home, the laughter of a child that would fill the silence. The dream that had seemed so far away, so impossible, now felt within reach, but still, they trod lightly, knowing that this dream had been shattered before.

Yet in their hearts, a seed of faith had been planted—a faith that dared to rise again, even in the face of past heartbreak. Could this be the child that would finally fulfill their long-awaited dream? They didn't know the answer yet, but for the first time in a long time, they allowed themselves to believe in the possibility of a miracle. So, they held on—held on to each other, held on to God's promises, and held on to the hope that this time, the dream they had carried for so long would finally come to life.

Sterling completed his seminary requirements, and by June 1969, they returned to Louisiana. On September 1, 1969, after years of heartache, Jean Miller gave birth to a healthy, beautiful baby girl—JoBeth, their miracle baby. She was carried to full term, and for the first time, Sterling and Jean held the fulfillment of God's promise in their arms. The scripture that had once been words on a page was now a living reality: God had provided what they needed, exactly when they needed it. Their hearts over-flowed with gratitude and awe at the goodness of God.

But the story wasn't over.

In Ephesians 3:20 (NKJV), God promises that He is able to do "exceedingly abundantly above all that we ask or think." Sterling and Jean had asked for one child. But thirteen months later, on November 9, 1970, Jean gave birth to their second miracle baby— Jay Miller. Once again, God had not only answered their prayer but had exceeded their wildest hopes.

THOSE DREAMS,

THE ONES

THAT STIR DEEP

WITHIN

YOUR SOUL,

ARE NOT THERE

BY ACCIDENT.

The Millers' hearts were full, their arms no longer empty. The legacy of faith Sterling had carried in his heart, the dream of passing that faith down to the next generation, was alive and thriving. God had not only given them one child but had blessed them with two—a double portion, a tangible reminder of His goodness and faithfulness.

Sterling, Jean, JoBeth, and Jay—the two miracle babies. Together, they would walk into the future, into the dreams God had prepared for them, into a legacy of faith that would inspire generations. What once seemed impossible was now their reality. God had redeemed their brokenness, restored their joy, and given them far more than they could have ever imagined.

In the end, their story wasn't just about two children. It was about a God who keeps His promises, a God who is faithful even when hope seems lost. As the Millers looked into the eyes of their miracle babies, they knew this truth with all their hearts: God never fails.

Never let go of the dreams that God has placed in your heart. Those dreams, the ones that stir deep within your soul, are not there by accident. They are divine seeds planted by the Creator, and though the path to seeing them fulfilled may be long and filled with challenges, know that God's timing is always perfect.

There will be days when the journey feels overwhelming, when the obstacles seem insurmountable, and when doubt threatens to consume your every thought. The dream that once burned so brightly in your heart may feel distant, obscured by the weight of fear and discouragement. But in those moments—those moments when the world whispers to you to give up, to settle, to move on—stand firm. God has not forgotten the promises He made to you.

Think of Joseph, whose dreams were met with betrayal and imprisonment, or David, who was anointed king but spent years running from Saul before he ever sat on the throne. They were men who held on to their dreams when everything around them screamed for them to let go. Yet, through every trial, God was working behind the scenes, preparing them for the fulfillment of His promises.

The same God who brought Joseph from the pit to the palace and who raised David from a shepherd to a king is the God who is working in your life right now. Proverbs 16:9 says, "In their hearts humans plan their course, but the LORD establishes their steps." Even when your plans seem to fall apart, know that God is orchestrating something far greater than you could ever imagine.

Do not be fooled by the silence. God is always working, even when you can't see it. Romans 8:28 reminds us that "all things work together for good for those who love God and are called according to His purpose" (author paraphrase). The setbacks, the closed doors, the delays—they are all part of the process. He is shaping you, refining you, and preparing you for the moment when that dream becomes reality.

And His timing is perfect. Though the waiting may feel unbearable at times, it is in the waiting that God does His most powerful work. He is preparing you for something greater than you could ever have imagined. Your dream may be big, but God's plan is bigger. Trust that what you are waiting for is worth it.

YOUR DREAM

MAY BE BIG,

BUT GOD'S

PLAN IS BIGGER.

TRUST THAT

WHAT YOU

ARE WAITING FOR

IS WORTH IT.

There will be moments of testing, moments when everything seems to be falling apart, but it is often in those moments that God is closest. Do not give up. Do not let go of the dream He has placed in your heart. When it feels like you've reached the end of your strength, that's when God steps in with His. Isaiah 40:31 promises us that "those who hope in the LORD will renew their strength. They will soar on wings like eagles; they will run and not grow weary, they will walk and not be faint."

So, hold on. Keep pressing forward. Even when the nights are long and the journey is hard, know that God is faithful. He sees you. He knows your heart. He is the author of your dreams, and He will not abandon the work He has started in you.

Your dream is not over. It is just beginning, and when God brings it to fulfillment, it will be far more beautiful, far more powerful, and far more glorious than you ever imagined. Hold tight to the One who gave you the dream, and trust that He is working all things together for good.

In the end, it is not the dream itself that sustains you, but the God who walks with you through every step of the journey—and He will not fail.

CHAPTER 12

IF MY MOM DIES

Jean Miller was not just extraordinary—she was irreplaceable. A woman whose love for people crossed every boundary, transcended every division, and reached into the darkest corners of the earth. She was a bright light in every place she stepped foot, whether it was a bustling city or a remote village. If there were souls in need, Jean was there, ready to pour out her heart, share the message of Jesus, and leave an indelible impact on everyone she encountered.

She didn't just travel; she ventured into the unknown, undeterred by danger or distance. Whether it was smuggling Bibles into Communist China alongside Marilyn Hickey, building a church in the war-torn streets of Latvia after the fall of the Soviet Union, or walking the sun-scorched barrios of Mexico, there was no place she deemed too far or too desolate. If people were there, Jean was there too, driven by a fire that couldn't be quenched, a passion to spread the love of Jesus to the ends of the earth.

Closer to home, Jean's love for people took her through the most crime-ridden streets of Lafayette, Louisiana. She walked through neighborhoods others feared, knocking on doors not to clean up the streets but to reach the hearts inside those homes.

She didn't care about the litter or the leaves—she knew those things would return. No, she saw a greater need—the need for Jesus. She believed if she could just reach one soul, it would last forever. And she did—again and again.

Jean wasn't just a woman of action—she was a force of nature, a builder of people, a nurturer of faith, and a mentor to countless souls. Where my father, Sterling, poured his energy into constructing the physical buildings of TFC, Jean was busy building something even more profound—the hearts of the people inside those walls.

She had a rare gift: the ability to see beyond the surface, to recognize the potential in people before they saw it in themselves. Jean knew that while brick and mortar were essential, it was the living, breathing souls within those walls that would make the ministry thrive. With every bit of love and wisdom she poured out, Jean was laying a foundation that would stand the test of time, one that would grow and flourish in ways no one could have imagined.

Through her weekly Bible studies, Jean touched thousands of lives. These gatherings weren't just about opening the Scriptures—they were about opening hearts. She had a way of breaking down the complexities of faith and making them deeply personal, speaking directly into the lives of those who sat before her. Jean's teachings weren't just lessons; they were life-giving truths that inspired people to step into their God-given callings. She poured into women, men, children, and families, investing her time, her wisdom, and her prayers into each one.

What made Jean truly remarkable was that she didn't just talk about faith—she lived it. Her life was a testament to the power of trusting in God, even in the midst of unimaginable hardship. She didn't just teach about the promises of God; she showed others how to stand on them. Jean's own journey of faith, marked by perseverance and grace, became a blueprint for those around her. She led by example, demonstrating that true strength isn't found in avoiding challenges but in walking through them with unshakable faith.

Jean was more than a pastor's wife. She was a mother to many, a spiritual guide who helped others navigate their own faith journeys. She could sense when someone was struggling, and without hesitation, she would take them under her wing, offering not just advice but the kind of love that made people feel seen and valued. It wasn't unusual for people to come to her burdened and leave feeling lighter, not because their problems had disappeared, but because they had been reminded of the God who carries them through.

Her impact was far-reaching, rippling through generations. The seeds she planted through those Bible studies have grown into a ministry that touches countless lives today. TFC didn't just grow because of the buildings Sterling erected—it grew because Jean nurtured the hearts inside, ensuring that faith took deep root in each person who crossed her path.

Jean's legacy is more than the sum of her words or actions. It's found in the lives she transformed, in the countless people who found hope, healing, and purpose through her ministry.

From those humble beginnings in 1973, TFC and Lafayette Christian Academy blossomed into thriving ministries. By 1980, the sanctuary was bursting at the seams, and new buildings seemed to spring up every year. The gymnasium, the classrooms, the community—it all grew under their watchful eyes and faithful prayers. The work was exhilarating, the church and school expanding beyond what anyone could have imagined.

In 1990, fresh out of Bible school, I returned home to Lafayette, ready to step into the family legacy. For two decades, I had watched from the front row as my parents led with integrity and faith. Now, I was ready to take my place. My dad began teaching me the nuts and bolts of ministry—how to buy land, build buildings, and balance budgets. But my mom? She taught me something far deeper—how to love people with passion, how to preach with conviction, and how to draw out the best in others.

The year 1990 marked my official entry into the ministry, and I quickly found myself part of something larger than I had ever imagined. TFC was growing, and so was I. Every day, I soaked up lessons from my parents—Sterling and Jean were no longer just my mom and dad, but my mentors. I saw firsthand what made them the "real deal." Their private conversations mirrored their public declarations. Their integrity was unwavering. Their love was genuine.

But in March of 1992, everything changed.

It was a bright Sunday morning, and as usual, I met my dad in his office before service. But there was something different in his demeanor—something heavy. He mentioned, almost offhandedly, that my mom had been feeling ill over the weekend and wouldn't be at church. Immediately, my heart sank. Jean Miller not at church? That was unheard of.

Later that day, she was rushed to the hospital. A tumor had ruptured in her abdomen, and by the time we arrived, she was barely conscious. The doctors moved quickly, stabilizing her as best they could, but the news was grim. Surgery was scheduled for the next morning, and the outlook wasn't good. The doctors told us she had lost so much blood that they weren't sure she would survive the operation.

I'll never forget the moment when the surgeon walked us into her pre-op room. My dad, my sister, and I stood there, staring at the woman who had always been the pillar of strength in our lives. Now, she lay weak and pale, barely able to open her eyes. The doctor, his face etched with concern, gave us a moment to say our goodbyes. He didn't think she would make it.

We huddled around her, holding hands, tears streaming down our faces as my dad prayed. But even in her weakened state, my mom had one more message for each of us. She reached for my dad's hand, her voice barely a whisper, and said, "Sterling, promise me, no matter what happens, you won't quit." She turned to JoBeth, my sister, and said the same. Then, she grabbed my hand, her grip surprisingly strong, and said, "Jay, promise me you won't quit. Stay the course. God's got a plan for you. I'm going to be all right."

Those words shook me to my core. The doctors rushed her into surgery, and we were left waiting, hearts heavy with fear. As I paced the halls, my mind raced. I was angry—angry at God, angry at the situation, angry that someone like my mom, who had given everything for others, was now lying on an operating table fighting for her life. Why her? Why now?

I found myself in a small bathroom, locking the door behind me, and for the first time in my life, I was ready to confront God. Staring at my reflection in the mirror, I said, "God, if my mom dies...." but then I stopped. I couldn't finish the sentence because I remembered her last words to me—*don't quit.*

NO

MATTER

WHAT

HAPPENS,

STAY

THE

COURSE.

In that tiny bathroom, I made a decision that would shape the rest of my life. I bowed my head and said, "God, if my mom dies, I'm going to spend the rest of my life loving You, serving You, and building Your kingdom. I'm just a servant. You are the King."

No matter what happens, stay the course. Those words are simple, but they carry profound meaning, especially in the life of a Christian. The journey of faith is not a sprint but a marathon, filled with challenges, setbacks, victories, and growth. As believers, we are called to endure, to hold on to the promises of God, and to trust that He is guiding us, even when the road ahead seems uncertain or difficult.

Throughout the Bible, we see stories of men and women who faced overwhelming odds, yet they remained faithful and stayed the course. Think about Noah, who was ridiculed for building an ark when no rain was in sight, but he trusted God's instruction. Abraham, who left everything he knew, set out on a journey without knowing his destination, simply because God said, "Go." Joseph, who endured betrayal, slavery, and imprisonment, never lost sight of the dreams God had given him. These stories remind us that God is faithful, and our faithfulness to Him, even when things are hard, will bear fruit.

The apostle Paul, who experienced more than his share of hardships—shipwrecks, beatings, imprisonment—wrote in 2 Timothy 4:7, "I have fought the good fight, I have finished the race, I have kept the faith." Paul's life was not easy, but he knew that what mattered most was finishing the race, staying true to his calling, and remaining faithful to the God who had called him. That same calling extends to each of us today. God has placed a unique mission and purpose in our lives, and no matter what happens, we are to stay the course, trusting that He will guide us through every storm.

Life often throws us unexpected challenges. Whether it's a personal loss, a financial setback, a health crisis, or an emotional struggle, it can feel tempting to give up or lose hope. But in these moments, it's crucial to remember that God is still in control. Even when circumstances look bleak, God is at work, weaving together a plan that will ultimately bring about His glory and our good.

Staying the course doesn't mean we won't have questions or doubts along the way. It's natural to wonder why things are happening as they are, but even in those moments of doubt, we are invited to lean into God's promises. In Proverbs 3:5-6, we are encouraged to, "Trust in the LORD with all your heart and lean not on your own understanding; in all your ways submit to him, and he will make your paths straight." Trusting God requires surrendering our limited understanding and believing that He knows the way, even when we cannot see it ourselves.

Remember that staying the course is not something we do in our own strength. Philippians 4:13 (BSB) says, "I can do all things through Christ who gives me strength." It is Christ who empowers us, strengthens us, and equips us to endure whatever comes our way. His grace is sufficient, and His power is made perfect in our weakness (2 Corinthians 12:9).

So no matter what happens—stay the course. God is faithful. He will not abandon you. The trials you face today are temporary, but the work God is doing in and through you has eternal significance. Keep running the race, keep fighting the good fight, and one day, like Paul, you too will be able to say, "I have finished the race; I have kept the faith."

THE TRIALS

YOU FACE TODAY

ARE TEMPORARY,

BUT THE WORK

GOD IS DOING

IN AND

THROUGH YOU

HAS ETERNAL

SIGNIFICANCE.

Jean made it through the surgery. She made a miraculous recovery. Seven days later, I drove her and my dad home from the hospital, grateful beyond words. God had granted us twenty-one more years with her—twenty-one more years to see her continue her ministry, plant churches, and impact lives across the globe.

In those twenty-one extra years, Jean helped plant three churches—one in Mexico, one in Texas, and one in Moss Bluff, Louisiana. She continued to walk through the same streets and the same neighborhoods, ministering with the same fiery passion, and every soul she touched left with a piece of Jean's heart, her love, and her unwavering faith in God.

But that moment, in that hospital, changed me forever. I knew then that no matter what life threw at me, I would never quit. My mom's legacy, her faith, her unwavering commitment to God—it lives on, not just in me, but in everyone she touched.

And so, I press on. For her. For God. For the calling that will not quit.

CHAPTER 13

WHAT WILL YOU PASS DOWN?

December 1968. The cold winds of Dallas swept across the city, but Sterling Miller felt an inner warmth that night—a fire that couldn't be extinguished. He had been waiting for this moment, praying fervently for a word from God, a word that would bring clarity and direction, and finally, it came. In the stillness of that night, God whispered a promise into Sterling's heart, one that would carry him for the next thirty years of his life and ministry.

It wasn't just any scripture—it was 1 Corinthians 1:7 (WB): **"So that you come behind in no gift."** But to Sterling, it was more than a verse—it was a direct and personal word from God. The promise was simple, yet powerful: "When you need it, it'll be there." Those words sank deep into Sterling's soul, solidifying a faith that would be tested time and time again.

Sterling didn't know then the full weight that promise would carry, nor the countless mountains it would move in the years to come. At that moment, all he knew was that the promise was from God—and that was enough. It wasn't about understanding how or when; it was about trusting the One who had spoken it.

The promise wasn't just a fleeting hope; it was a lifeline, a seed of faith planted deep within Sterling's heart. He couldn't have foreseen the incredible ways God would fulfill it, but he believed, and that belief was enough to set in motion a journey far greater than he could ever imagine.

As the years unfolded, the promise began to take shape in ways that neither Sterling nor Jean could have expected. They had always dreamed of a family—of children filling their home with laughter, of a legacy built on faith and love—but after years of heartbreak, miscarriage, and devastating loss, that dream had begun to fade. The pain of unfulfilled hope weighed heavily on their hearts, and the future they had once envisioned seemed increasingly out of reach. Each loss was a wound that cut deeper than the last, and with every passing year, their hope dimmed.

But God is a keeper of promises. Even in the midst of their sorrow, He was working behind the scenes, weaving together a story of redemption and fulfillment that they couldn't yet see. His promise was not forgotten. In the fullness of His timing, the impossible became possible. God honored His word, and into their lives came two miracle babies—gifts that defied the odds, children born out of faith, perseverance, and the relentless love of a faithful God.

These children weren't just the fulfillment of a long-held dream; they were living testimonies to the power of God's promise. Every cry, every laugh, every milestone reached was a reminder that no matter how long the wait or how deep the sorrow, God's word never returns void. The once-empty home became filled with the sounds of life, the echoes of joy bouncing off walls that had been silent for so long.

WHEN GOD

MAKES A PROMISE,

NO MATTER

HOW IMPOSSIBLE

IT SEEMS,

HE WILL

FULFILL IT.

ALWAYS.

Sterling and Jean's journey wasn't just about becoming parents—it was about witnessing firsthand the faithfulness of a God who moves mountains. A God who turns mourning into joy and who fulfills His promises in ways that exceed our wildest expectations. What started as a fragile hope, spoken in faith, had grown into a reality far more beautiful than they could have imagined. Those two miracle babies were more than just answers to prayer; they were the embodiment of God's unwavering faithfulness, proof that when He speaks, He is always true to His word.

As Sterling reflected on the years that had passed, he realized that the promise had carried far more weight than he ever could have known. It didn't just bring children into his life—it brought restoration, healing, and a deeper understanding of who God is. The journey had been long, the mountains steep, but God had been with them every step of the way, and through it all, Sterling knew one thing for certain: when God makes a promise, no matter how impossible it seems, He will fulfill it. Always.

The next trial came in the form of land. They had found the perfect property for their future ministry, but they had only sixty dollars in their bank account. It seemed impossible, but once again, God honored His word. The property was theirs—a miraculous gift. But then came another hurdle: they needed a building. With no resources left, they were unsure how it would happen, and yet, within weeks, a building was donated. Sterling and Jean stood in awe of how God's promise continually showed up when they needed it most.

As a young boy, I had the privilege of watching all of this unfold. I had a front-row seat to the miraculous life and ministry of Sterling and Jean Miller. I saw firsthand how God always sent the right people, the right resources, and the right provisions at the right time. The promise of "when you need it, it'll be there" was not just a comforting idea—it was the heartbeat of everything they did.

But the greatest test of that promise came in 1980, during the final weeks of completing the new church auditorium. Sterling and Jean had a burning vision to take the church deeper into the things of God, to make it a life-giving place where people from all walks of life could encounter God. They wanted to reach the highways and byways, to stretch the ministry beyond its walls.

The congregation was mostly on board, but there were doubters, and worse, the budget was running on fumes. With less than $1,000 left and a building still incomplete, Sterling was stretched to his limit. His faith was being tested like never before.

Then, a wealthy man from the congregation approached Sterling with a check in hand. The amount was staggering—$100,000. It was five times what was needed to finish the project, an incredible windfall. But the check came with conditions. The man made it clear: "You can have this money, but you must abandon this new vision. Don't move forward with these changes. It won't work."

In one hand, Sterling held the check—the answer to his financial worries. In the other, he held the hammer—the symbol of the unfinished work that still required so much more faith. For a moment, the weight of the decision must have been crushing, but Sterling didn't flinch. Without hesitation, he looked the man in the eye and said, "I appreciate your offer, but this ministry—my calling—it's not for sale."

His words were like thunder. I stood there, a boy watching my father turn down what seemed like a lifeline. But it wasn't about money. It was about obedience to the call of God. Sterling chose to trust in the promise that had carried him this far. "I'd rather trust God at His word and fail," he told the gentleman, "than to put my trust in your money."

The man walked away, and with him, the check. But God wasn't done. In the days that followed, several families from Texas relocated to Lafayette and found their way to our church. They didn't just bring resources—they brought hands and hearts. They painted, laid tile, and hung drywall, and by the time the work was complete, so was the funding. Every need was met, down to the last penny. God had once again honored His promise.

That story was just one of many. I could recount tale after tale of how God's provision showed up in the most impossible of circumstances. For over fifty years, the promise of 1 Corinthians 1:7 had been woven into the very fabric of our ministry. It wasn't just a scripture—it was a lifeline.

God's promises are just as alive today as they were throughout the pages of Scripture. The same God who spoke to Abraham, Moses, and David is still speaking to us today, offering promises of hope, guidance, and provision. In a world filled with uncertainty, God's promises stand firm as an anchor for our souls. His faithfulness does not change, and His word remains unshakable.

In 2 Corinthians 1:20 (NKJV), we are reminded, "For all the promises of God in Him are Yes, and in Him Amen, to the glory of God through us." This means that every promise God has made is affirmed and fulfilled in Christ. Whether we're trusting God for provision, peace, healing, or wisdom, His promises are still active, living, and relevant for today's believers.

Even when circumstances seem bleak, we can trust in God's unchanging nature. His promises do not depend on our situation but on His eternal character. The promise of His presence, His provision, and His ultimate victory are just as true today as they were thousands of years ago.

As followers of Christ, we are called to stand on these promises with faith, knowing that God is faithful, and His word will never fail.

On March 31, 2002, that promise became my own. It was Easter Sunday, a day already charged with celebration, but this Easter was different. After twenty-nine years of faithful ministry to TFC and Lafayette Christian Academy, Sterling and Jean Miller passed the mantle of leadership to me and my wife, Tessy. I was thirty-one years old, and our three small children were in the front row, watching with wide eyes. For the first time in nearly three decades, a new senior pastor was being called. The weight of that responsibility was immense, but so was the promise that came with it.

With the mantle came the same anointing that had carried my father. The same promise of 1 Corinthians 1:7: "When you need it, it'll be there."

The next years saw the church grow in ways I had only dreamed of. We opened a new elementary building in 2007, and by 2009, we had expanded the property from the original 2.5 acres to over fifty acres. God continued to move, but the tests never stopped. When we needed a new high school and sports complex, we estimated a budget of $4 million. We saved diligently for years, but when the time came to hire a contractor, the numbers were staggering. The project was estimated at $10 million—far beyond what we had prepared for.

I was devastated. I felt like I had failed. I walked the length of our fifty-acre campus that day, tears streaming down my face, crying out to God. And in that low moment, I heard His voice again: "Jay, do you remember my promise? Do you remember 1 Corinthians 1:7? It's still in effect."

Encouraged, I made a call to the owner of the property next to us, a piece of land we had leased for ball practice for years. I asked if he would sell us a small portion—just three acres. To my surprise, he said, "No. I don't want to sell you three acres. I want to sell you all fifteen acres and the buildings on it."

It was a miracle. We bought the entire property for $1.2 million. The renovations were estimated at $2.2 million—bringing the total to exactly $4 million, the number we had originally budgeted for.

God had once again shown up when we needed Him most.

Now, as I look at my five sons—three of whom stand beside me in ministry today—I am deeply reminded of the legacy my father passed down to me. It wasn't just a legacy of words or traditions; it was a legacy of unwavering faith, a legacy built on trusting God's promises through every season, no matter how impossible the road ahead seemed. My father's faith was a foundation, a mantle that I hope, one day, to pass down to all my sons. But more than anything, I want them to inherit that same unshakable trust in God that has carried our family through the storms and into the miracles.

FAITH IS

A LEGACY THAT

TRANSCENDS TIME,

AND IT'S OUR

RESPONSIBILITY

TO STEWARD

THAT GIFT WELL.

Because they're watching. The next generation is always watching—taking in not just what we say, but how we live, how we respond to challenges, and how we hold onto God when the world tells us to give up. What we pass down to them today will shape not only their future but the lives of generations to come. Faith is a legacy that transcends time, and it's our responsibility to steward that gift well.

So, ask yourself: "*What will I pass down?*" Will it be fear or faith, doubt or trust in the One who has never failed? What you pour into the next generation will ripple through eternity. Let it be a legacy of faith, built on the foundation of God's promises, that will inspire them to walk boldly in their calling.

CHAPTER 14

WHEN PRAYERS DON'T WORK

It was January 2012 when the opportunity arose. A ten-acre tract of land, located right next to a parcel TFC had purchased just a few years earlier, was suddenly up for grabs. In my mind, it felt like an easy decision. The land was ideally positioned—landlocked in a way that gave us leverage. With the two properties combined, we could potentially make a commercial sale one day, should the need arise.

The price? Unbelievably low. Far below what it was worth. The deal felt right, almost like it had been hand-delivered. There was just one problem.

A glaring, unavoidable problem.

A line of towering, steel power poles—seventy feet high—cut straight through the heart of the property. These massive, ugly poles loomed over the land like unwanted giants, their presence impossible to ignore. But for the price per acre, I felt an odd sense of peace. It was a risk, but one I was willing to take.

So we bought it.

The plan was simple. Turn around and sell it. With its highway frontage, it was the perfect commercial piece of property. It should have been an easy transaction. Valuable. Desirable. A no-brainer.

But it wasn't.

Over the next six years, five different buyers put contracts on that land. Each time, hope sparked within me, only to be extinguished when the buyers backed out—one after the other—and every time, the reason was the same: those unsightly power lines. No one wanted a piece of land marred by those towering metal structures.

I started to hate those power lines.

Without them, we could have sold the property five times over. Instead, every contract that fell through became a personal defeat, a reminder that my hands were tied by something beyond my control. I would drive past the property and see those poles standing there, mocking me, reminding me of all the prayers that seemed to go unanswered.

And I prayed—a lot.

"Lord, we really need this land to sell. We could use the money elsewhere, where it's needed." I prayed earnestly, reminding God of how much we could accomplish if He would just help us get this one thing done. But every time, all I got in return was silence.

For eight long years.

When it feels like your prayers are echoing into the void, unanswered and seemingly ignored, it's so easy to grow weary and disheartened. You pour your heart out to God, pleading, hoping for a breakthrough, but what you're met with feels like silence. The delay can feel unbearable, and in those quiet, painful moments, doubt creeps in. You may even start to ask yourself, *Does God really hear me? Does He see my pain? Does He care?*

But let me assure you of this: God hears *every* word. Even when heaven seems quiet, God is not absent. His silence is not indifference; it's a divine pause, a moment where trust is built in the waiting. He is working in ways we cannot see, and His plans often unfold in the spaces where we feel most uncertain. God's timing is perfect, even when it doesn't align with ours. His delays are not denials, and His silence is often a space where He is preparing something greater than we could ever imagine.

In these moments of questioning and waiting, it's essential to remember that God's ways are higher than ours. Isaiah 55:8-9 reassures us, *"'For My thoughts are not your thoughts, neither are your ways My ways,' declares the Lord. 'As the heavens are higher than the earth, so are My ways higher than your ways and My thoughts than your thoughts.'"* What seems like a delay or an unanswered prayer is often God orchestrating something far beyond our understanding. His perspective is eternal, while ours is finite. He sees the full picture—the beginning, the middle, and the end—while we only see a single frame of the story.

In those moments when you feel like giving up, know that God is not distant. He is closer than your very breath, collecting every tear and hearing every cry. He is working in the unseen, and His answers are on the way, even if they don't come in the form or timing we expect. Trust that His silence is not abandonment, but a season where faith is forged, and endurance is strengthened.

So, hold fast to hope. Continue to pray, continue to trust, and believe that even in the silence, God is at work. His ways are higher, His plans are greater, and His love for you is deeper than you could ever comprehend. He has not forgotten you, and He never will.

GOD HEARS

EVERY WORD.

EVEN WHEN

HEAVEN SEEMS

QUIET,

GOD IS

NOT ABSENT.

Sometimes, God's silence is His way of working behind the scenes, aligning circumstances, preparing hearts, or protecting us from something we can't yet see. He knows the end from the beginning, and His delays are not denials. Often, what we interpret as unanswered prayer is God's way of saying, "Trust Me. I have something better in store."

Remember, God's timing is perfect. In Galatians 6:9, we are encouraged not to grow weary in doing good, for at the proper time, we will reap a harvest if we do not give up. So, hold on to your faith. Keep praying, even when it's hard. Stay rooted in His promises, trusting that He will answer in His way, at the right time.

When you feel like your prayers are going nowhere, know that God is listening. His silence could be setting the stage for something greater than you ever imagined. Keep trusting. Keep believing. God's answer is on the way.

The land sat there, unsold, and I started to question everything. Was I praying wrong? Was God not listening? Why wasn't anything changing? And those poles—those hideous poles—became the focus of my frustration. I remember praying, half in jest, "Lord, if You won't sell the land, at least send a storm to blow those ugly power lines down."

But no storm came. The poles stood firm, and my prayers felt like they were hitting a wall of silence.

By October 2021, my expectations had hit rock bottom. So, when an attorney from Breaux Bridge called, asking to discuss the land, I assumed it was just another dead end. Another potential buyer, another disappointment.

Reluctantly, I returned his call, already bracing myself for the letdown.

The attorney's voice was calm as he began. "Pastor, I have some news about your property," he said, his tone neutral, almost casual. "It's about the land with the power lines."

Great, I thought. Here we go again. "What is it?" I asked, trying to sound interested.

"Well," he began, "the lease on those power lines is about to expire."

I almost didn't hear him correctly. "Excuse me? What lease?"

"The power lines," he repeated. "They were installed in 1921 under a one-hundred-year lease agreement, and that lease is about to expire. The utility company is looking to renew it."

A one-hundred-year lease? From 1921? I blinked in disbelief. That was nearly two decades before my father, Sterling, was even born. How could this be? I'd never heard of such a thing.

"I don't want to renew," I said, a little too quickly. "Those poles are the reason we can't sell the land."

There was a brief pause, and then the attorney spoke again. "You may want to rethink that," he said, and I could hear a smile in his voice. "The utility company is offering $600,000 to renew the lease."

My breath caught. Six hundred thousand dollars?

"And," he added, "if you can agree to the terms before the end of the year, they're willing to throw in a $300,000 bonus. That's a total of $900,000."

The phone nearly slipped from my hand.

For a moment, I couldn't speak. I sat there, trying to wrap my head around what he was telling me. A lease that had been signed a century ago—back in 1921—was about to become the biggest blessing we could have imagined. Nine hundred thousand dollars for power lines I had hated with every fiber of my being.

When I hung up the phone, I was overwhelmed. All these years, I had been praying—pleading—for the land to sell, and all these years, God had been silent. But now, looking back, I realized something profound: His silence wasn't neglect. It wasn't a dismissal of my prayers. It was His way of protecting me. Of preserving something far greater than I could have ever envisioned.

You see, God knew the timeline. He knew about that one-hundred-year lease long before I ever set foot on that property. While I was busy begging for a quick sale, He was orchestrating something much bigger, something I couldn't even see, and now, we were receiving far more than any sale would have ever brought—and we still owned the land.

So, the next time you drive through Lafayette, Louisiana, near Exit 101, I'll be the first to point out some of the prettiest seventy-foot power lines you've ever seen. And yes, I love them now.

Because those power lines are a reminder. A reminder that even when it feels like your prayers are falling on deaf ears, God is listening. He's working. He knows the timeline. And sometimes, silence is His greatest answer.

In the silence of your darkest hour, when the weight of the world presses down and your heart aches with unanswered prayers, know this: God hears your cry. Every tear you've shed, every whispered plea—He's captured them all. His silence is not absence, but preparation. He's moving behind the scenes, weaving a greater plan than you can see. Just as the dawn breaks after the deepest night, so will His answer come. Hold on. The heavens are not deaf to your cries; they are working to bring forth a miracle at the perfect time. God hears you—always.

Keep trusting. God knows when the lease is going to expire.

THE HEAVENS

ARE NOT DEAF

TO YOUR CRIES;

THEY ARE WORKING

TO BRING FORTH

A MIRACLE AT

THE PERFECT TIME.

CHAPTER 15

I'M IN HAWAII

The summer of 2006 dawned like any other in Louisiana, with the warmth of the sun creeping through the windows of Jean's home. Just as she had done every morning for decades, Jean woke up early, ready to greet the day. Her routine was sacred. By 6 a.m., without fail, she would be found in her recliner—Bible in one hand, notebook and pen in the other. It was her time with God, and nothing interrupted it. She approached each morning as if it were Christmas, filled with the same excitement of a child about to open a gift, eager to see what treasure God had hidden for her in His Word that day.

It wasn't that she hadn't read the Bible before. In fact, she had gone through it cover to cover many times, each time with fresh eyes, knowing that there was always something new to discover, something more to learn. I watched her all my life, sitting in that chair, studying and delighting in the Word of God. Her joy was infectious, and her faith immovable.

But on that particular morning, something was different. Jean felt it in her bones—a subtle, unsettling whisper that her body wasn't quite responding as usual. There was a legacy of kidney failure in her family, and though she couldn't be sure, a quiet unease began to take root in her heart. She scheduled a doctor's appointment, and after a few tests, the call came: Jean's kidneys were functioning at less than 20 percent. Dialysis was now on the table, a road she had seen other family members walk.

But Jean—strong, faithful Jean—didn't falter. Her faith didn't waver, not for a second. She chose to trust in the same God who had carried her through so many trials before. The family stood with her, unified in prayer, believing for the miraculous. Jean didn't begin dialysis right away; she stood on her faith, believing that God could intervene, just as He had done so many times before. She had seen Him do the impossible, and she wasn't ready to give up on the God of miracles.

The waiting room of life can be one of the most difficult places to inhabit. You've prayed, you've trusted, and you've placed your hope in God. Yet, the breakthrough hasn't come. The healing hasn't appeared. The miracle you've longed for remains out of reach. As days stretch into weeks and weeks into months or even years, the question arises: how do you stay strong while waiting for a miracle?

For many, waiting feels like a form of suffering. It stretches the soul in ways nothing else can. We often wonder if God hears our prayers, if He has forgotten us, or if perhaps He's decided not to act. The truth, however, is that waiting is not a sign of God's absence, but rather an invitation to draw closer to Him, to deepen our faith, and to experience His sustaining grace.

Through it all, Jean continued to live her life fully. She was at church every Sunday, critiquing my sermons with the love only a mother can give—always supportive but never afraid to tell me the truth. She loved on her grandchildren, spending time with them and teaching them the promises of God. They adored her. Since the arrival of her first grandchild, she insisted on being called "Grandmother." There would be NO substitutions. My son, Sterling, her first grandchild, called her "Monie"—a name born out of a toddler's mispronunciation, but one that stuck. From that day on, she was "Monie" to all the grandchildren. The title Grandmother was never mentioned again.

Even as her health began to deteriorate, Jean's faith only grew stronger. She lived her life as if nothing had changed. Every Sunday, she sat in her pew, Bible in hand, still expecting God to show up, still believing in the promise of healing.

Then, in 2009, the time came when Jean's body couldn't hold out any longer. Dialysis became inevitable. Three days a week, for hours at a time, she sat in that chair at the clinic, hooked up to the machine that was now doing what her kidneys no longer could. But Jean didn't waste a moment. Even there, she shared her faith. Every person who sat near her heard about the goodness of God. She prayed for people, shared her testimony, and led many to Christ. The dialysis clinic became her mission field.

The last week of Jean's life was spent in a hospital bed at General Hospital in Lafayette. My dad sat beside her from dawn till dusk, holding her hand, loving her with the kind of quiet devotion that had marked their marriage for over fifty years. My sister and my wife, Tessy, took turns sitting by her bedside throughout the nights. We knew the time was coming, and yet, even in those final moments, there was peace. We were releasing her into the arms of the One she had trusted her entire life.

On the morning of January 4, 2012, Jean Hunt Miller lay still, her breath shallow and her body weary from the journey.

Suddenly, her eyes fluttered open, just for a moment, as if she were glimpsing something beyond this world. A single tear escaped down her cheek as if it carried the weight of a lifetime of love, faith, and battles fought. Then, with quiet grace, she took her final breath.

As she slipped from this life into the arms of Jesus, the weight of her earthly journey finally lifted. Her worn and tired body, having endured so much, was now at peace—no longer bound by pain, illness, or the limitations of this world. She was free, stepping into eternity where there was no more sorrow, no more suffering, and no more tears. She left behind the world, but she did not leave us empty-handed.

What she left behind was far greater than memories. She left us with a legacy of faith, of strength, and of love that will echo through generations. Her faith was not a quiet, hidden thing—it was bold, fierce, and unapologetically lived out for all to see. She didn't just talk about trusting God; she demonstrated it in every moment, whether in times of abundance or through trials that would have shaken the strongest of hearts. Through every hardship, her faith stood tall, unwavering, a beacon of hope to those who watched her closely.

Her strength wasn't merely physical—it was a deep inner resilience that came from walking hand-in-hand with God through every valley and mountaintop. Even when her body grew weak, her spirit remained unshakable, grounded in the promises of God that she clung to with all her heart. She faced life's challenges with courage, her eyes always fixed on Jesus, and she taught us to do the same.

LIVING YOUR

FAITH OUT LOUD

ISN'T ABOUT

BEING PERFECT

OR HAVING

ALL THE ANSWERS.

And her love—it was boundless. She loved fiercely, selflessly, and with a grace that could only come from a heart surrendered to God. Her love wasn't just something she spoke about; it was something she lived. Whether through her comforting words, her caring touch, or her constant prayers for those she held dear, her love left an indelible mark on all who knew her.

But the greatest gift she left us was her faith—a faith that transcends time. It wasn't just a private belief; it was the foundation of her entire life, one she shared openly and boldly. Her faith was her testimony, her compass, and her guiding light. It was the reason she could face every storm with peace and every joy with gratitude. She passed that faith down to us—not as a mere inheritance, but as a charge, a calling, to live with the same boldness, to trust God with the same unwavering conviction, and to love others as Christ has loved us.

Though she has left this world, her influence remains. Her faith continues to inspire, her strength continues to encourage, and her love continues to ripple through the lives she has touched. She is gone, but the legacy she left behind—of faith, strength, and love—will carry on, lighting the path for all of us who remain. We carry her with us, not just in our hearts but in how we live our own lives, with the same bold faith and enduring love that she so freely gave.

Jean taught us that living your faith out loud is a courageous act of letting God's light shine through you in every aspect of your life. As Christians, we are called to be "a city on a hill" that cannot be hidden (Matthew 5:14-16). This means our faith should be visible in how we speak, act, and treat others. It's about reflecting Christ's love, not just in words but in how we live every day.

Living your faith out loud isn't about being perfect or having all the answers. It's about showing the world the hope and joy that comes from knowing Jesus, even in the midst of challenges. When you boldly share your faith, whether through kindness, prayer, or standing for truth, you become a beacon of God's love. Trust that God will use your life to inspire others and draw them closer to Him. This is exactly what Jean taught us every single day.

My children still talk about "Monie"—how she would plead the blood of Jesus over them, how she taught them to love God with all their hearts. One morning, I walked in to find my oldest son, Sterling, at five years old with all his brothers lined up like soldiers, and he was channeling his inner "Monie" with the most serious face. He raised his hand and declared, "I plead the blood of Jesus over all of y'all!" I couldn't help but laugh because, honestly, with that bunch, they probably needed it! It was like a mini prayer revival in our living room—led by a five-year-old who had clearly learned from the best.

My boys still laugh about the time Regan, my son, fell out of the tree at Monie's house. My mom had tried to downplay it, saying it was "just a little scratch." As I rushed him to the ER, his little scratch required seventy-two stitches. That was Monie— always seeing the best, always filled with hope, no matter the situation. Even now, every time we see Regan's eight-inch scar on his leg, we think of Monie!

Every now and then, when the family gathers and those stories about Monie start flowing, I find myself slipping back into my own memories. Memories I had for forty-two years with her as her son. Forty-two years of learning from her, being loved by her and seeing her live out her faith in the most extraordinary ways, and though she's no longer with us, her legacy lives on in every one of us.

As for Micah, he still cracks up every time he hears the phrase, "I'm not here; I'm in Hawaii." That's what Monie would always say when she answered his phone calls, as if she had a secret beach hideaway no one knew about. And every time I hear it, I can't help but smile. Sure, Hawaii sounds nice, but let's be real—Monie's in heaven now, and she's upgraded to a destination far more glorious than any island paradise!

CHAPTER 16

HAPPY MOTHER'S DAY, JEAN!

How long are you willing to wait for a dream to come true? How long can hope continue to burn in your heart when day after day, year after year, your prayer seems to go unanswered, lost in the silence of heaven? What do you do when the delay stretches into months, then years, and still nothing? Can you hold on when the dream begins to feel like a distant memory, when the very thing you long for feels impossibly out of reach?

Would you wait forty-two years for your miracle? Would you continue to believe, even when the passing time seems to mock your faith? What if each passing day adds weight to the burden you carry, threatening to crush your spirit beneath the weight of unanswered prayers? Would you still trust? Would you still believe that the God who planted the dream in your heart is faithful to fulfill it, no matter how long it takes?

Waiting isn't easy. It's the space where doubt creeps in, where discouragement whispers that maybe it's time to give up, that maybe your dream wasn't meant to be. But waiting is also the crucible where faith is forged, where perseverance and trust are refined. It is in the waiting where we learn that faith isn't just about receiving; it's about enduring. It's about believing in God's goodness even when you can't see His hand moving.

Imagine holding on to a dream for forty-two years. Forty-two years of unanswered prayers, of wondering, of aching for the fulfillment of a promise. Could you continue to hope, to trust that the delay is not denial, but divine timing? The weight of that waiting can feel unbearable, like a heavy stone pressing down on your heart, yet it is in this tension that God strengthens our faith and deepens our trust in Him.

What if your miracle is just on the other side of the next prayer, the next day, the next step of faith? What if the very thing you've been waiting for is about to break through, but you've grown too weary to keep believing? Would you let go too soon, or would you keep holding on, trusting that the God who began a good work will be faithful to complete it?

Waiting for a dream to come true is never easy, but the question remains: How long are you willing to wait? Because in the waiting, God is working—preparing you, shaping you, and refining your character for the very thing He has promised. And when the fulfillment comes, after all the years of holding on, it will be sweeter than anything you could have ever imagined.

So, would you wait forty-two years for your miracle? Would you trust God to carry you through the silence, through the doubt, through the moments when the dream feels distant? Would you dare to believe that even in the delay, God is preparing something far greater than you could have dreamed on your own? The waiting is not wasted. Your faith, if held firm, will bring forth a miracle in God's perfect time. Hold on—your miracle is worth the wait.

FAITH

ISN'T JUST

ABOUT

RECEIVING;

IT'S ABOUT

ENDURING.

In October of 1967, the sound of the gavel crashing down in the courtroom was like a thunderclap that shattered Sterling and Jean Miller's world. The judge's decision was final—JoJo and Henry, the two boys they had loved as their own, would return to their biological parents. The family they had hoped to build was being torn away, leaving behind only a few fading photographs and the ache of loss.

That moment felt like the death of their dream. Yet even in their heartbreak, God's grace pierced through the darkness. On September 1st, 1969, a new light entered their lives with the birth of their daughter, JoBeth. After twelve long years of praying and waiting, the Miller family was finally growing. It was a promise fulfilled, a glimmer of hope.

But life, as it so often does, delivered another devastating blow. Early in 1970, word came that Henry, at just eight years old, had been diagnosed with leukemia. The disease moved swiftly, and before they could even process the news, Henry was gone. Although Sterling and Jean had respected the court's order and maintained no contact with the family, they couldn't let Henry pass without saying goodbye.

With heavy hearts, they requested permission to attend the funeral and they were granted five brief, solitary minutes to pay their respects. The small, quiet funeral home was completely empty. Only Henry's tiny casket remained. Jean and Sterling held hands, overwhelmed by the memories that flooded back—the laughter, the prayers, the joy of those two precious years. Jean, filled with both gratitude and sorrow, thanked God for the time they had with Henry.

Sterling's hand trembled as he gently placed it on Henry's small, lifeless fingers. His mind drifted back to the little boy's earnest prayers, the ones Henry had whispered with unwavering faith, asking God that his "Daddy" would come to church with him. Sterling had never gone. The weight of that broken promise now hung heavy in the air, the silence around them louder than any prayer ever spoken. Sterling now fully recognized the weight of Henry's faith.

Jean's hands shook as she leaned down, her breath catching with the weight of her grief. Tears streamed down her face, falling onto Henry's pale skin as she pressed a trembling kiss to his forehead. Her voice cracked as she whispered through the sobs, "One day . . . I'll see you again, son." The words hung in the air, fragile and full of hope, but crushed by the unbearable sorrow of that moment, as if she was trying to cling to a promise that felt so far away.

As they left the funeral home in silence, hearts heavy, they returned to their home, where Jean's mother, Vivian, was caring for their nine-month-old daughter, JoBeth. Holding JoBeth in his arms, Sterling thanked God for the gift of life, even in the midst of loss. That night, they dug through a box in the closet, finding the few photos they had of JoJo and Henry. Jean gently placed one of the boys in an old frame, and from that day forward, no matter where they lived, that photo remained on display in their home—a reminder of love, loss, and faith.

As much as Henry's passing left a void, new life emerged later that same year. On November 9th, 1970, Jean gave birth to their son, Jay Sterling Miller. A year marked by tragedy also became one marked by the promise of new beginnings. From then on, the framed photograph of JoJo and Henry traveled with the Millers wherever they went, a permanent fixture in their family's story.

For as long as I can remember, the picture of JoJo and Henry hung in our home, always there, quietly watching over us. It sat alongside the portraits of my parents, JoBeth, and me, a constant reminder that our family was made up of more than just the faces we saw every day. That picture wasn't just an image—it was a piece of our family, a story that spoke of both heartache and hope, one that my parents shared openly with anyone who asked.

We grew up knowing what that picture represented—the pain and loss that came with it, the bittersweet memory of the two boys who had been in our parents' arms for a brief time but never left their hearts. JoJo and Henry were part of the fabric of our family, not because we saw them every day but because their presence lingered in our home, in the stories my parents told. That picture was more than a photograph—it was a reflection of the love that never faded despite the years that separated us.

As children, we felt the weight of that picture. We knew it wasn't just about the sorrow of what had been lost, but about the enduring hope that remained. Our parents never shied away from sharing the story of JoJo and Henry—the joy they had brought into our family, and the deep ache of having to let them go. But more than anything, our parents shared the unwavering belief that even in loss, God was still faithful. They believed that love, even when tested by unimaginable pain, could still endure.

That picture became a symbol in our home—not just of loss, but of resilience. It reminded us daily of the strength our parents carried, and of the faith that sustained them through every trial. We learned, through their example, that heartache doesn't have the final say. The picture of JoJo and Henry was a constant testament to the truth that love endures beyond separation, and that hope, even when it seems fragile, is never fully extinguished.

That picture, quietly hanging in our home, spoke volumes about who we are as a family. It was a reminder that even in the darkest seasons, there is always hope. And though JoJo and Henry were not physically with us, their presence was felt in every corner of our lives, woven into the fabric of our family's story. They will always be a part of us, and their memory will forever remind us of the enduring power of love and the unbreakable strength of hope.

For forty-two years, my mother, Jean, prayed a simple, unwavering prayer—that one day, JoJo would walk through the doors of TFC, his wife on one side and children on the other, and sit proudly with the entire Miller family in church. Every time she looked at that picture, her prayer grew stronger. It was a prayer of faith, of hope against hope, whispered through the decades.

On January 4th, 2012, my mother passed away. Over her forty-four years of ministry, she had seen countless prayers answered. She had witnessed miracles unfold before her eyes. But one prayer remained unanswered in her lifetime—that forty-two-year prayer for JoJo.

Then, just four months later, on May 13th, 2012, the miracle finally arrived. JoJo, his beautiful wife beside him and his two children in tow, walked into TFC and sat on the front row. My father, Sterling, sat on one side of him, and I stood on the other.

A forty-two-year dream had come to life—a dream my mother had never seen in her lifetime but one that had never left her heart. As JoJo and his family took their seats, I couldn't help but believe that somehow, in the mystery of heaven, my mother witnessed that moment. The prayer she had carried for so long had finally come to pass.

That day, I learned something profound about prayer. Our prayers, if rooted in faith, can outlive us. Even if we don't see the answer with our own eyes, we must keep praying, keep believing, and keep trusting. I had always heard that there's power in prayer, but on May 13th, 2012, I experienced that power firsthand. I experienced a prayer that outlived the one who spoke it.

The answer to my mother's prayer had finally arrived. Even if it took forty-two years. Even if it came four months after her death.

Oh, and by the way, May 13th, 2012 was Mother's Day!

Happy Mother's Day, Jean.

CHAPTER 17

WE BUILT A FAMILY

July 15, 1994—a date that will always be engraved in my heart. It was the day I married my high school sweetheart, Teresa Lasseigne. The girl I knew, deep down, was the one long before she even realized it. Our journey to that moment wasn't without its challenges—life has a way of testing love in ways you don't expect—but somehow, our love proved itself time and again. It was the kind of love that rises above the noise, the pressures, and the uncertainties of life. No matter what came our way, we found our way back to each other. Love, real love, always will.

For years, I had been bold enough to say that I'd ask a girl to marry me even if we weren't dating, and deep inside, I always knew who that girl would be. It might sound presumptuous to some, but I always believed that Tessy was the one for me. It was written in my heart long before it ever unfolded.

In April 1994, I decided to put that belief into action. I didn't just want to propose to Tessy in a quiet, intimate setting. No, I wanted it to be a public declaration—a moment shared with the community we loved. One Sunday morning, in front of our entire congregation, I orchestrated a proposal she would never forget. Tessy was escorted to the front of the stage, unaware of what was about to happen. I walked down the aisle, heart racing, the eyes of hundreds of people following my every step. The room was thick with anticipation.

As I stood before her, the woman I'd always known would one day be my wife, I could feel the weight of the moment. Tessy had no idea what was about to unfold. I glanced at her father, Mr. Darrell Lasseigne, standing in the audience, his eyes locked on mine. Just days before, we had met in private—a necessary conversation before this moment could take place. I had asked for his blessing, and with a serious look and a shovel in his hand, he gave it, warning me, "Don't break my daughter's heart."

That warning echoed in my mind as I looked at him again, standing there, silent but watchful. His eyes said it all: *This is your moment, kid. Don't blow it. Take care of her. Don't break her heart.* With a deep breath, I proposed to Tessy in front of God, our family, and our church, and when she said yes, it felt like everything in my life had aligned in that single moment. We were beginning the journey we had always dreamed of.

The years since that day have been filled with the beauty and complexity that marriage brings. I can't say that I've never caused Tessy any heartache—because that's simply not true. There have been moments when my words or actions have brought her to tears, times when life felt heavier than we could bear. But through every trial, we found our way back to each other. Grace and forgiveness became our foundation. In every season, we extended those gifts to one another, and it's what has kept us strong, even when the world felt uncertain.

Two and a half years later, on November 24, 1996, our first son was born. We named him Jay Sterling Miller II, after his grandfather and me. That moment, the moment I held my son for the first time, was something Tessy and I had talked about for years. We had always dreamed of starting a family together, and this was the beginning.

Our family didn't stop there. By April 5, 2006, the Miller family was complete—five sons. Five boys, each one a unique story, a unique journey. Tessy's license plate still reads "BOYZRUS," and that pretty much sums up the world we've lived in for the last three decades.

Raising five boys was an adventure of epic proportions—equal parts joy, chaos, and a permanent state of exhaustion. There were days I felt like a referee in a never-ending wrestling match, and others where I was convinced we were running a small circus instead of a family. But, oh, the memories we've made! They are etched into my soul like battle scars of parenthood, each one telling a story of its own.

There were the legendary summer vacations in the RV, where the boys somehow turned every campsite into their personal playground—and where I learned that five boys in a confined space can turn even the most peaceful national park into a war zone of sibling rivalry. The ski trips were an annual test of our sanity, with snowball fights escalating into full-blown battles and the occasional "accidental" tumble down the slopes. And who could forget the football games under the lights, where half the fun was watching them compete, and the other half was praying they'd make it through without breaking any bones— or the bleachers.

Beach trips were another highlight. Sand in every imaginable place, laughter that carried on the ocean breeze, and the occasional seagull daring to swoop down and steal a snack—it was a perfect blend of fun and chaos. But those moments, those wild and wonderful adventures, were just the surface of the memories we built together.

The real gift, the moments I treasure most, were the everyday happenings, the ones that didn't require a special trip or a big event. The noisy mornings, when the house came alive like a roaring train station, everyone scrambling for breakfast, shoes, and some semblance of order. The impromptu wrestling matches that could break out at any moment—sometimes over the TV remote, sometimes just because someone looked at someone else "the wrong way." Those wrestling matches were like an unscheduled family tradition, and I'm still not entirely sure how the furniture survived.

And let's not forget the logistics of feeding five growing boys. It was like running a full-time cafeteria. We went through five gallons of milk, six dozen eggs, and four loaves of bread a week—just to keep everyone satisfied. There was a stretch where I bought diapers for ten straight years. When people would ask me, "What do you want for your birthday or Christmas?" my answer was always the same: "A Walmart gift card, please." Feeding that many mouths felt like an Olympic event, and let's not even talk about laundry!

Picture five boys sitting around the table, sharing stories of their day, usually involving something broken, something lost, or someone in trouble. Laughter would erupt between bites, and as much as I loved the beach trips and football games, it was these moments—this daily rhythm of chaos and connection—that I cherish most. The simple act of being together, even in the mess and noise, was the true gift.

HER HEART

GUIDED OUR HOME

IN WAYS

THAT MY

LEADERSHIP

NEVER COULD.

Yes, raising five boys was an adventure, but it was also the greatest joy. The memories we made—the big trips, the small moments, the laughter, and the sleepless nights—are woven into the very fabric of who we are. Looking back, I wouldn't trade a single moment of it. Well, maybe the moments when they thought they could go fast enough to keep the 4-wheelers on top of the water of the pond. But even those, in hindsight, have their place in the beautiful, chaotic tapestry that is our family's story.

Through it all, Tessy was the true backbone of our family. She wasn't just their mother; she was their everything. She was their chef, their chauffeur, their counselor, their confidant. She built a home where love wasn't just something we said, it was something we lived. Talk badly about her boys, and you would see her fierce protection in full force; those claws would come out. But as much as she loved them, she ruled with grace and wisdom. There were moments when we didn't agree on how to handle certain situations, and she would look at me and say, "Jay, please, let me be the mom." She had an intuition about them that I could never fully understand, and I trusted her completely. Her heart guided our home in ways that my leadership never could.

We worked hard to teach our boys the importance of keeping Christ at the center of their lives. At times, it felt like our words were bouncing off the walls, especially during those teenage years, when they seemed more interested in football than faith. But we stayed faithful, trusting that the seeds we were planting would take root. And they did.

Today, three of our boys serve full-time at TFC. Sterling, married to Hannah, serves as our CFO. Regan and his wife, Wendy, lead our student and college ministries. Jansen and his wife, Kaitlyn, are the pastors of our first impressions team. Micah is in college and serves faithfully on our worship team and is leading an FCA campus college group, while Britt, our youngest, is a senior in high school and helps wherever he can as well as serves on the worship team.

Every day, as Tessy and I drive onto the church campus at 223 Stone Ave, we are reminded of the incredible journey we've been on. To see our family working together, building God's kingdom hand in hand—it's more than we ever could have dreamed. I can't imagine that in 1973, when Sterling and Jean started out on this incredible journey, they would have imagined all of this.

There's a memory that stands out from the summer of 2002. I was at a pastor's roundtable in Atlanta, and one of the keynote speakers shared about his adult children, all of whom were doing incredible things for God. My boys were still young at the time, but something stirred inside of me. After the session, I raised my hand and asked, "What did you do to help your children become so successful in their adult lives now?" The speaker looked surprised. He told me no one had ever asked him that before, but he shared five principles that guided his family. He said that there were many things that he would like to go back in time and change; however, there were five things he did that he would never change. I came home and couldn't wait to share them with Tessy. We implemented those five principles immediately, and they became the pillars of how we raised our boys. And they worked—those principles shaped the men our sons have become.

WE DIDN'T

JUST BUILD

A HOUSE—

WE BUILT

A FAMILY.

Now, with Britt preparing to step into his next season of life, our house is quieter than it once was. We're no longer buying gallons of milk and loaves of bread by the truckload. The laundry is less, and our evenings are a bit more peaceful. But as we walk through our home, we're reminded of the memories we've made and the family we've built. We didn't just build a house—**we built a family.**

There are still more stories to be told, more memories waiting to be made, more miracles to mention. The chapters of this journey aren't yet complete. But for now, I'll set down my pen, letting the ink dry for just a moment. As I sit here, I hear the unmistakable sound of tiny footsteps—soft and eager—climbing the stairs to my office. It's Beckham Jules Miller, our first grandchild, just eighteen months old. His giggles fill the air as he toddles toward me, unaware of the weight of the legacy he's stepping into, a legacy shaped by faith, perseverance, and love.

The journey isn't over. No, it's only just begun. I'll scoop him up, just as I did with my own boys, and hold him close, feeling the pulse of new life, of new beginnings. I'll whisper to him the same lessons Sterling and Jean poured into my children. The legacy doesn't end with us; it continues, one generation at a time, growing deeper and richer with each life touched by the faith that has carried us this far.

As I look into Beckham's wide blue eyes, filled with curiosity and innocence, I know that this is only the beginning of his own faith journey, his own two and a half acres of life yet to be discovered. The baton is being passed, and with it, the responsibility is to keep building lives, families, and futures.

The legacy continues. The promise lives on. And maybe, just maybe, your own two-and-a-half acres of faith journey begins today. Take that first step and see what God will do.

If you're ready to take your first step into your own two-and-a-half acres of faith, let me help by leading you in a simple but powerful prayer:

"Lord Jesus, I come to You as I am—broken and in need of a Savior. I need a fresh start, and I ask You to heal my broken heart. Lead me, guide me, and help me trust You every step of the way. I surrender my life to You. Amen."

This prayer is more than just words; it's the beginning of something extraordinary, the first step in trusting God to write a story of hope and purpose in your life. No matter where you are or what you've been through, He's ready to meet you right where you are and take you further than you ever imagined.

Your two-and-a-half acres of faith may look different from mine, but it will be just as meaningful, just as miraculous, and just as life-changing. I can't wait to hear your story and celebrate the incredible journey God is preparing for you. Take that step, trust Him, and watch what He can do!

ABOUT THE FAMILY CHURCH

Since 1973, The Family Church (TFC) in Lafayette, LA, has grown from humble beginnings on just 2.5 acres into a vibrant, multi-racial congregation that now thrives on over one hundred acres. With over 22 million in state-of-the-art facilities, Pastors Jay and Tessy Miller lead this life-giving church, serving more than 1,800 passionate members. TFC is a place for the whole family—featuring a cutting-edge Kidzworld, exciting youth services, and a dynamic college ministry. With a heart for reaching every generation, TFC is building lives, families, and futures, transforming the Lafayette area and beyond with hope and faith.

ABOUT LAFAYETTE CHRISTIAN ACADEMY

L afayette Christian Academy (LCA) is a premier private Christian school located in Lafayette, LA, serving over 1,200 students from K4 through twelfth grade. Known for its commitment to excellence, LCA provides a dynamic and nurturing environment where faith and education unite. With a highly dedicated and passionate staff, LCA delivers a curriculum designed to challenge, inspire, and equip students for success both academically and spiritually.

The school's motto, "Building Lives—One Student at a Time," reflects its core mission of shaping future leaders through a holistic approach to education. LCA also boasts a championship-caliber athletic program, empowering students to excel in sports while building character, teamwork, and discipline. Whether in the classroom, on the field, or in the community, LCA is a place where students are encouraged to reach their full potential and embrace their God-given purpose.

At LCA, students grow in faith, develop critical skills, and prepare to make a positive impact on the world. With a history of academic excellence, strong moral values, and a winning spirit, LCA is shaping the next generation of champions for Christ.

AUTHOR BIO

Jay Miller is the senior pastor of The Family Church (TFC) in Lafayette, Louisiana. The son of Sterling and Jean Miller, Jay grew up witnessing the transformative power of faith to overcome adversity. He now carries forward that legacy, guiding others with the same biblical principles. Under his leadership, TFC and LCA continue to grow, inspiring countless individuals to walk in faith and hope.

Jay is a dynamic speaker who leaves his listeners filled with hope, passion, and renewed belief. His authentic and compassionate nature uplifts and empowers individuals, leaving them with practical steps to live with purpose and faith.